THEOSOPHY

THEOSOPHY

BY
ANNIE BESANT

GYAN

ISBN: 978-81-212-1898-6 (HB)
First Published, 1912
Published, 2018
Published by

Gyan Publishing House
5, Ansari Road
Daryaganj, New Delhi-110002
Phone: 011-47034999, 9811692060
www.gyanbooks.com
E-mail: books@gyanbooks.com

Printed at: G. Print Process, Delhi.

CONTENTS

THEOSOPHY

INTRODUCTION

THEOSOPHY is derived from two Greek words—*Theos*, God; *Sophia*, Wisdom—and is therefore God-Wisdom, Divine Wisdom. Any dictionary will give as its meaning: "A claim to a direct knowledge of God and of Spirits," a definition which is not inaccurate, though it is scanty and affords but a small idea of all that is covered by the word, either historically or practically. The obtaining of "a direct knowledge of God" is—as we shall see in dealing with the religious aspect of Theosophy—the ultimate object of all Theosophy, as it is the very heart and life of all true Religion; this is "the highest knowledge, the knowledge of Him by whom all else is known"; but the lower knowledge, that of the knowable "all else" and the methods of knowing it, bulk largely in Theosophical study. This is natural enough, for the supreme knowledge must be gained by each for himself, and little can be done by another, save by pointing to the way, by inspiring to the effort, by setting the example; whereas the lower knowledge may be taught in books, in lectures, in conversation, is transmissible from mouth to ear.

THE MYSTERIES

This inner, or esoteric, side of religion is found in all the great faiths of the world, more or less explicitly declared, but always existing as the heart of the religion, beyond all the dogmas which form the exoteric side. Where the exoteric side propounds a dogma to the intellect, the esoteric offers a truth to the Spirit; the one is seen and defended by reason, the other is grasped by intuition—that faculty "beyond the reason" after which the philosophy of the West is now groping. In the religions that have passed away it was taught in the "Mysteries," in the only way in which it can be taught—by giving instruction how to pursue the methods which unfold the life of the Spirit more rapidly than that life unfolds in natural and unassisted evolution; we learn from classical writers that in the Mysteries the fear of death was removed, and that the object aimed at was not the making of a good man—only the man who was already good was admissible—but the transforming of the good man into a God. Such Mysteries existed as the heart of the religions of antiquity, and only gradually disappeared from Europe from the fourth to the eighth centuries, when they ceased—for want of pupils. We find many traces of the Christian Mysteries in the early Christian writers, especially in the works of S. Clement of Alexandria and of Origen, under the name of "The Mysteries of Jesus". The condition of high morality was made here, as in the Greek Mysteries: "Those who for a long time have been conscious of no transgression . . . let them draw near." Indications of their origin and existence are found in the New Testament, in which the Christ is said to have taught His disciples secretly—"Unto you it is given to know the mysteries of the Kingdom of God, but to others in parables"—and these teachings, Origen maintains, were handed down in the Mysteries of Jesus; S. Paul also declares that "we speak 'wisdom' among them that are 'perfect'"—two terms used in the Mysteries. Islām has its secret teachings—said to have been derived from Ali, the son-in-law of the Prophet Muhammad—to be found by meditation and a discipline of life, methods taught among the Sūfīs. Buddhism has its Sangha, within which, again by meditation and a discipline of life, the inner truth is to be found. Hindūism, both in its scriptures and its current beliefs, asserts the existence of the supreme and the lower knowledge, the latter to be gained by instruction, the former, once more, by meditation and a discipline of life. It is this which makes the supreme knowledge "esoteric"; it is not deliberately veiled and hidden away, but it cannot be imparted; it can only be gained by the unfolding of a faculty, of a power to know, of a mode of consciousness, latent in all men, but not yet developed in the course of normal evolution. This shows itself sporadically in the Mystic, often in erratic fashion, often accompanied with hysteria, but, even then, is none the less an indication—for the clear-sighted and unprejudiced—of a new departure in the long evolution of human consciousness. It is brought to the surface sometimes by exceptional purity: "the pure in heart . . . shall see God." Startling irruptions of it into ordinary life are seen in such cases of "sudden conversion" as are recorded by Prof. James.[1] The spiritual consciousness is a reality; its witness is found in all religions, and it is stirring in many to-day, as it has stirred in all ages. Its evolution in the individual can only be gently and deliberately forced, ahead of normal evolution, by the meditation and the discipline of life alluded to above. For esotericism in religion is not a teaching, but a stage of consciousness; it is not an instruction, but a life. Hence the complaint made by many, that it is elusive, indefinite; it is so to those who have not experienced it, for *only that which has been experienced in consciousness can be known to consciousness*. Esoteric methods can be taught, but the esoteric knowledge to which they lead, when successfully followed and lived, must be won by each for himself. We may help to remove obstacles to vision, but a man can only see with his own eyes.

[1] *Varieties of Religious Experience.*

THE PRIMARY MEANING

Theosophy is this direct knowledge of God; the search after this is the Mysticism, or Esotericism, common to all religions, thrown by Theosophy into a scientific form, as in Hindūism, Buddhism, Roman Catholic Christianity and Sūfīsm. Like these, it teaches in a quite clear and definite way the methods of reaching first-hand knowledge by unfolding the spiritual consciousness, and by evolving the organs through which that consciousness can function on our earth—once more, the methods of meditation and of a discipline of life. Hence it is the same as the Science of the Self,[1] the Science of the Eternal,[2] which is the core of Hindūism; it is "the Knowledge of God which is Eternal Life" which is the essence of Christianity. It is not a new thing, but is in all religions, and hence we find the late eminent Orientalist, Max Müller, writing his well-known work on *Theosophy, or Psychological Religion.*

THE SECONDARY MEANING

Theosophy, in a secondary sense—the above being the primary—is the body of doctrine, obtained by separating the beliefs common to all religions from the peculiarities, specialities, rites, ceremonies and customs which mark off one religion from another; it presents these common truths as a consensus of world-beliefs, forming, in their entirety, the Wisdom-Religion, or the Universal Religion, the source from which all separate religions spring, the trunk of the Tree of Life from which they all branch forth.

The name Theosophy, which, as we have said, is Greek, was first used by Ammonius Saccas, in the third century after Christ, and has remained ever since in the history of religion in the West, denoting not only Mysticism, but also an eclectic system, which accepts

[1] Ātma-vidyā. [2] Brahma-vidyā.

truth wherever it is to be found, and cares little for its outer trappings. It appeared in its present form in America and Europe in 1875, at the time when Comparative Mythology was being used as an effective weapon against Christianity, and, by transforming it into Comparative Religion, it built the researches and discoveries of archæologists and antiquarians into bulwarks of defence for the friends of religion, instead of leaving them as missiles of attack for its enemies

COMPARATIVE MYTHOLOGY

The unburying of ancient cities, the opening of old tombs, the translation of archaic manuscripts of both dead and living religions, proved to demonstration the fact that all the great religions which existed and had existed resembled each other in their most salient features. Their chief doctrines, the outlines of their morality, the stories which clustered round their founders, their symbols, their ceremonies, closely resembled each other. The facts were undeniable, for they were carved on ancient temples, written down in ancient books; the further research was carried, the bulkier grew the evidence. Even among the most degraded tribes of savages, traces were found of similar teachings, traditions of sacred truths overlaid by the crudities of animism and fetishism. How to explain such similarities? what their bearing on Christianity? "Evolution" was then the "open sesame" of Science, and the answer to these questions was not long delayed. Religion had *evolved;* from the dark ignorance of primeval savages, who personified the powers of the Nature they feared, had evolved the inspiring religions and the splendid philosophies which had enthralled and civilised mankind. The medicine-men of savages had been glorified into Founders of religions; the teachings of Saints and Prophets were the refining of the hysterical babblings of half-epileptic visionaries; the synthesis of natural forces—a synthesis wrought out by man's splendid intellect—had been emotionalised into God. Such was the answer of Comparative Mythology to the alarmed questionings of men and women who found their houses of faith crumbling into pieces around them, leaving them exposed to the icy winds of doubt. At the same time Immortality was threatened, and though intuition whispered: "Not all of me shall die," physiology had captured psychology, and was showing the brain as the creator of thought—thought, which was born with the brain, grew with it, was diseased with it, decayed with it; did it not finally die with it? Agnosticism grew and flourished; what could man know, beyond what his senses could discover, beyond what his intellect could grasp? Such was the condition of educated thought in the last quarter of the nineteenth century. The younger generation can scarcely realise that veritable "eclipse of faith".

COMPARATIVE RELIGION

Into that Europe Theosophy suddenly came, asserting the Gnosis as against Agnosticism, Comparative Religion against Comparative Mythology. It declared that man had not exhausted his powers in using his senses and his intellect, for that beyond these there were the intuition and the sure witness of the Spirit; that the existence of these powers was a demonstrable fact; that the testimony of the spiritual consciousness was as indubitable as that of the intellectual and the sensuous. It admitted all the facts discovered by archæologists and antiquarians, but asserted that they were susceptible of quite other explanation than that given by the enemies of religion, and that while the facts were facts the explanation was only a hypothesis. It set over against this hypothesis another, equally explanatory of the facts—that the community of religious teachings, ethics, stories, symbols, ceremonies, and even the traces of these among savages, arose from the derivation of all religions from a common centre, from a Brotherhood of Divine Men, which sent out one of its members into the world from time to time to found a new religion, containing the same essential verities as its predecessors, but varying in form with the needs of the time, and with the capacities of the people to whom the Messenger was sent. It was obvious that either hypothesis would explain the admitted facts. How should a decision between them be reached? Theosophy appealed to history: it pointed out that the palmy days of each religion were its early days, and that the teachings of the Messenger were never improved on by the later adherents of the faith, whereas the contrary must have been the case if the religion had been produced by evolution; the Hindūs founded themselves on their Upaniṣhads,[1] the Zoroastrians on the teachings of their Prophet, the Buddhists on the sayings of the Lord Buddha, the Hebrews on Moses and the Prophets, the Christians on the teachings of the Lord Christ, the Muhammadans on those of their great Prophet. Later religious literature consisted of commentaries, dissertations, arguments, not of new departures, more inspiring than the original. Inspiration is ever sought in later days in the sayings of the Founder, and in the teachings of His immediate disciples. Manu, Vyāsa, Zarathushtra, the Buddha, the Christ—these Figures tower above humanity, and command the love and reverence of mankind, generation after generation. These are the Messengers, the religions are their messages. Theosophy points to all these as the proofs that its hypothesis is the true explanation of the facts, is no longer a hypothesis, indeed, but is a truth affirmed by history. Against this splendid array of Messengers with their messages, Comparative Mythology cannot bring one single proof from history of a religion that has evolved from savagery into spirituality and philosophy; its hypothesis is disproved by history.

The Theosophical view is now so widely accepted that people do not realise how triumphant was the opposing

[1] Their most ancient literature, a part of the Vedas.

theory, when Theosophy again rode into the arena of the world's thought in 1875, mounted on its new steed, the Theosophical Society. But any who would realise the conditions then existing should turn to the literature of Comparative Mythology, published during the preceding century, from the voluminous works of Dulaure and Dupuis,[1] through Higgins' *Anacalypsis*, to the books of Hargrave Jennings, Forlong, and a dozen others, speaking with a positiveness that led the reader to believe that the statements made were based on facts, which no educated person could deny. Those who plunged into that labyrinth of discussions in their youth, who lost themselves in its endless and intricate windings, who saw their faith devoured by the Minotaur of Comparative Mythology, they know—and only they can know in its fullness—the intensity of the relief when the modern Ariadne—the much misunderstood and much maligned Helena Petrovna Blavatsky—gave them a clue which guided them through the mazes of the labyrinth, and armed them with the sword of the "Secret Doctrine"[2] with which to slay the monster.

It may be interesting to note, in passing, that old-fashioned Christianity—which believed that all mankind had descended from Adam, created 4004 B.C.—had preserved a tradition of a primeval revelation, given to Adam and carried by his posterity to all parts of the world; man, inheriting original sin from his ancestor, had corrupted this, but traces of it were to be found in the grains of truth hidden by the husks of "heathen" religions. This view, however, despite the germ of truth it contained, was quite out of court with educated people, who knew that the human race had existed for hundreds of thousands of years, at least, instead of for a span of six thousand.

[1] On phallic and sun worships.

[2] Mme. Blavatsky's monumental work, published in 1889.

UNITY OF RELIGIONS

The outcome of the whole position is that the fact of the community of religious belief is destructive to any religion which claims for itself a unique and isolated position; in such a position it is exposed to attack from all sides, and its claim is easily disproved. But this same fact is a defence, when all religions stand together, when they present themselves as a Brotherhood, children of one ancestor, the Divine Wisdom.

This view becomes the more satisfactory as we notice that each religion has its own special note, makes its own special contribution to the forces working for the evolution of man. As we notice their differences, in addition to their similarities, we feel that they reveal a plan of human education, just as when we hear a splendid chord we feel that a master-musician has combined the notes, with a full knowledge of the value of each. Hindūism proclaims the One Immanent Life in everything, and hence the solidarity of all, the duty of each to each, enshrined in the untranslatable word Dharma.[1] Zoroastrianism strikes the note of Purity—purity of surroundings, of body, of mind. Hebraism sounds out Righteousness. Egypt makes Science its word of power. Buddhism asserts Right Knowledge. Greece breathes of Beauty. Rome tells of Law. Christianity teaches the value of the Individual and exalts Self-Sacrifice. Islām peals out the Unity of God. Surely the world is the richer for each, and we cannot spare one jewel from our chaplet of the world's religions. Out of the fair spectacle of their varied beauty and the spiritual value of the variety, grows in our minds the sense of the reality of the great Brotherhood, and its work in the

[1] Dharma, translated as religion, duty, obligation, is more than these. It indicates the sum of a man's past evolution—all that has made him what he is—and the next steps which he must take in order to ensure his further evolution with the least possible delay and difficulty.

guidance of spiritual evolution. So deep a unity, so exquisite and fruitful a diversity, cannot be mere chance, mere coincidence, but must be the result of a plan deliberately adopted and strongly carried out.

METHOD OF STUDY

As the Theosophical system of thought is an immense, an all-inclusive, synthesis of truths, as it deals with God, the Universe, and Man, and their relations to each other, it will be best to divide its presentation under four heads, corresponding to a very obvious and rational view of Man. Man may be regarded as having a physical body, an emotional nature, and an intellect; and through these he, an eternal Spirit, manifests himself in this mortal world. These three departments of human nature, as we may call them, correspond to his great activities: Science, Ethics and Æsthetics, Philosophy.

(1) Through his senses Man observes the phenomena around him, and verifies his observations by experiments; through his brain he records and arranges his observations, makes inductions, frames hypotheses, tests his hypotheses by devising crucial experiments, and arrives at knowledge of Nature and understanding of her laws: thus he constructs sciences, the splendid results of the intelligent use of the organs of the physical body on the physical world. We must study Theosophy as SCIENCE.

(2) Man's emotional nature shows feelings and desires —feelings caused by contacts with the outside, contacts which give pleasure or pain; these arouse in him desires —cravings to re-experience the pleasure, to avoid the recurrence of the pain. We shall see, when we come to deal with these, that the deep-rooted yearning for Happiness, planted in every sentient creature, spurs him to place himself at last in harmony with law, that is, to do the Right, to refuse to do the Wrong. The expression of this harmony in life, in our relations with

others and in the building of ourselves, is Right Conduct. The expression of this same harmony in matter is Right Form, or Beauty. We must study Theosophy as MORALITY-ART.

(3) Man's intellect demands that his surroundings, both as regards life and matter, shall be intelligible to him; it demands order, rationality, logical explanation. It cannot live in a chaos without suffering; it must know and understand, if it is to exist in peace. We must study Theosophy as PHILOSOPHY.

(4) But these three, Science, Morality-Art, Philosophy, do not perfectly satisfy our nature. The religious consciousness persistently obtrudes itself in all nations, all climes, all ages. It refuses to be silenced, and will feed on the husks of superstition if denied the bread of Truth. The Spirit who is Man will not cease his search for the universal Spirit who is God, and God's answers—partial but with the promise of more—are religions. We must study Theosophy as RELIGION.

Under these four heads all the Theosophical teachings most important to human life and conduct may be presented. There remain: a few indications of the practical application of these to social problems, and a mere statement—for within the brief compass of this little book no more is possible—of the larger vistas of the past and the future opened up to us by Theosophy.

All divisions which seek to divide the really indivisible Spirit—the spark from the universal Fire—are unsatisfactory, and tend to veil from us the unity of the consciousness which is our Self. Senses, emotions, intellect, are but facets of the one diamond, aspects of the one Spirit. Spiritual life, Religion, should be a synthesis of Science, Morality-Art, and Philosophy—they are but facets of Religion. Religion should permeate all studies, as Spirit permeates all forms. Our Self is one, not multiple, albeit his overflowing life expresses itself in multitudinous ways. So although, for the sake of clarity, I divide my subject into parts, I would pray my reader to remember that classification is a means and not an end; that classifications are many, while consciousness is one; and that while, for lucid explanation, we may avoid confusing the persons, we should ever bear in mind that we must also avoid dividing the substance.

SECTION I

Theosophy as Science

The old way of study was to state universals, and to descend from them to particulars, and it remains the best way for serious and philosophic students. The modern way is to begin with particulars, and to ascend from them to universals; for the modern reader, who has not yet made up his mind to a serious study of a subject, this is the easier road, for it keeps the most difficult part for the last. As this little book is meant for the general reader, I follow this way.

Theosophy accepts the *method* of Science—observation, experiment, arrangement of ascertained facts, induction, hypothesis, deduction, verification, assertion of the discovered truth—but immensely increases its *area*. It sees the sum of existence as containing but two factors, Life and Form, or, as some call them, Spirit and Matter, others Time and Space, for Spirit is God's motion, while Matter is His stillness; both find their union in Him, since the Root of Spirit is His Life, and the Root of Matter is the universal Æther, the two aspects of the One Eternal, out of Space and Time.[1] While ordinary science confines Matter to the tangible, Theosophical science extends it through many grades, intangible to the physical, but tangible to the super-physical, senses. It has observed that the condition of knowing the physical universe is the possession of a physical body, of which certain parts have been evolved into organs of sense, eyes, ears, etc., through which

[1] See Section III., p. 54.

perception of outside objects is possible, and other parts have been evolved into organs of action, hands, feet, and the rest, through which contact with outside objects can be obtained. It sees that, in the past, physical evolution has been brought about by the efforts of life to use its nascent powers, and that the struggle to exercise an inborn faculty has slowly shaped matter into an organ through which that faculty can be more fully exercised. To reverse Büchner's statement: We do not walk because we have legs; we have legs because we wanted to move. We can trace the growth of legs from the temporary pseudopodia of the amœba, through the development of permanent protrusions from bodies, up to the legs of man, and they were all gradually formed by the efforts of the living creature to move. As W. K. Clifford said of the huge saurians of a past age: "Some *wanted* to fly, and they became birds." The "Will to live"—that is, to desire, to think, to act—lies behind all evolution.

The Theosophist carries on the same principle into higher realms, if such exist; and if consciousness is to know any other sphere [1] than the physical, it must have a body of matter belonging to the sphere it wants to investigate, and the body must have senses, developed by the same want of the Life to see, to hear, etc. That there should be other spheres, and other bodies through which those spheres can be known, is no more inherently incredible than that there is a physical sphere, and that there are physical bodies through which we know it. The Occultist—the student of the workings of the divine Mind in Nature—asserts that there are such spheres, and that he has and uses such bodies. The following statements—with one exception which will

[1] I use the word "sphere" to indicate the whole extent of matter belonging to a definite type, *i.e.* built of atoms of one sort. See under "Atoms" in Section VI. There may be several worlds in a sphere; thus the heaven-world is in the mental sphere. The word plane has been used in this sense, but it is found that people do not readily grasp its meaning.

be noted in its place—are made as results of investigations carried on in such spheres by the use of such bodies by the writer and other Occultists; we all received the outline from highly developed members of our humanity, and have proved it true step by step, and have filled in many gaps, by our own researches. We, therefore, feel that we have the right to affirm, on our own first-hand experience—stretching over a period of twenty-three years in one case, and twenty-five in another—that super-physical research is practicable, and is as trustworthy as physical research, and should be carried on in similar ways; that investigators are subject to errors, both in physical and super-physical spheres, and for similar reasons, and that these errors should lead to closer research and not to its discontinuance.

A TABLE OF CORRESPONDENCES

The following table presents a view of the spheres related to and including our earth, of the bodies used in investigating them, and of the states of consciousness manifested through them by their owner, the Man. The Eternal Man, a fragment of the Life of God, is called the Monad, a "oneness"; [1] he is verily a Son of God, made in His image, and expressing his life in three ways: by the aspect of Will, the aspect of Wisdom, the aspect of Creative Activity. He lives in his own sphere, a spark *in* the divine Fire, and sends down a ray, a current of his life, which embodies itself in the five spheres of manifestation. This ray, appropriating an atom of matter from each of the three higher of these spheres, appears as the human Spirit, reproducing the

[1] This is the statement, including what is said farther on about the Monad, noted above, as not having been verified by the writer's own observation. This highest Self is only made manifest to such as we are on rare occasions in a great downflow of dazzling light: in his own nature, in his own world, he is beyond the reach of any vision yet attained by any of us. Yet what we call our life is his, since he is the highest Self in each of us, "the hidden God"—as the Egyptians used to say.

three aspects of the Monad, of Will, Wisdom, and Creative Activity, and reveals himself, at a certain stage of evolution, as the human ego, the individualised Self; he begins his long journey as a mere seed of life, and, *never losing his identity*, moves through that long journey, unfolding all the powers of the Monad, that lie hidden within him, as the tree in the seed. As he conquers his kingdom of matter, his Parent-Monad pours down into him more and more life, and draws from him more and more knowledge of the worlds in which he lives. But the passing into the three highest manifested spheres is not enough for gaining full knowledge and full power in our Solar System; two yet remain, and the process of dipping down into matter goes on. The Spirit strengthens himself for his work by appropriating a molecule of the coarser matter of the lowest sphere he has so far entered, and links on to this an atom from the fourth manifested sphere of denser matter, and one from the fifth, the lowest, our physical sphere. He is to obtain bodies, formed round these permanently appropriated particles of matter, by which he may be able to know and act upon the five manifested spheres. We shall see that his lower bodies, forming what is called his Personality, are cast off at and after what we call death, and are renewed for each successive birth, while the higher, forming his Individuality, remain through his long pilgrimage—an important fact as bearing on the possibility of remembering the past. The above facts are tabulated opposite (see p. 25).

It may be asked: "What is the object of this descent into matter? What does the Monad gain by it?" Omniscient in his own sphere, he is blinded by matter in the spheres of manifestation, being unable to respond to their vibrations. As a man who cannot swim, flung into deep water, is drowned, but can learn to move freely in it, so with the Monad. At the end of his pilgrimage, he will be free of the Solar System, able to function in any part of it, to create at will, to move at pleasure. Every power that he unfolds through denser

	SPHERES.	BEINGS.		STATES OF CONSCIOUSNESS.	BODIES.
Unmanifested.	1. Divine.	Logos.		Divine Triplicity.[1]	....
	2. Monadic.	Human Monad.		Monadic Triplicity.[2] (Will, Wisdom, Activity.)	....
Manifested.	3. Spiritual.	Man, who is	An Immortal Individuality.	Spirit, individualised as Will.	Atom.
	4. Intuitional.	„ „		„ „ „ Intuition.	Intuitional.
	5. Mental.	„ „		„ „ „ Intellect.	Causal.
	„	„ who has	A Mortal Personality.	Mind.	Mental.
	6. Astral, or Emotional.	„ „		Desires and Emotions.	Astral.
	7. Physical.	„ „		Vitality.*	Physical.

* [As Vitality shows itself in two main forms in the Physical Body, the latter is functionally divided into two: Energising Vitality works through the finer part, called the Etheric Double, composed of the four physical ethers, and Automatic Vitality uses the denser part, composed of solids, liquids, and gases. These seven subdivisions of physical matter make up the physical sphere.][3]

[The student may find the Sanskrit terms useful, as they have been much employed in Theosophical literature, and the above are my own English equivalents: 1. Ādi; 2. Anupādaka; 3. Ātmā, or Nirvāṇa; 4. Buddhi; 5. Manas (adjective, mānasic); 6. Kāma; 7. Sthūla. The Buddhists use for Ādi, Mahāparinirvāṇa, and for Anupādaka, Parinirvāṇa.]

1 The Trinities of religions, the Three Persons of Christianity. As manifested in a Solar System They appear three by difference of function, seen from below. The whole Solar System may be called the Body of the Logos, and the Sun His physical Body, but they only embody a fragment of Him.

2 Man, "made in the Image of God". His aspects, Will, Wisdom, and Activity, or Power, Knowledge-Love, and Creativeness, are shown in the embodied reproduction of himself, as Will, Intuition, and Intellect.

3 The seven are named from below upwards: solid, liquid, gaseous, etheric, super-etheric, sub-atomic, atomic.

matter, he retains for ever under all conditions; the implicit has become explicit, the potential the actual. It is his own Will to live in all spheres, and not only in one, that draws him into manifestation.

THE PHYSICAL BODY

The actual unfolding of consciousness is best traced from below, for the physical body is the one which is first organised as its instrument for knowledge, and it unfolds itself by this in the physical world we know. The emotional nature stimulates the glands and ganglia of the physical body, and the mental enthrones itself over the cerebro-spinal system, and these proceed with their evolution in the invisible spheres through the stimulus obtained from the physical. We need not dwell on the evolution of the dense physical body, as that may be studied as physical science. Human consciousness is here automatic, the Man having no longer need to direct physical processes; they go on by habit, the result of long pressure from consciousness. The finer part of the physical body, the etheric double, permeates the dense, and extends a little beyond it over the whole surface; its proper sense-organs are vortices on its own surface, situated opposite (1) the top of the head, (2) the point between the eyebrows, (3) the throat, (4) the heart, (5) the spleen, (6) the solar plexus, (7) the base of the spine, (8, 9, 10) in the lower part of the pelvic basin; these last are not used, except in Black Magic. These vortices—technically called chakrams, wheels, from their appearance—are aroused into activity in the course of occult training, and form a bridge between the physical and astral spheres, so that the latter comes to be included within the activity of the waking consciousness. The health of its dense partner depends on the Vitality in the etheric double, which draws its energy directly from the Sun, and, in the part in contact with the spleen, divides this energy into streams, which it conveys to the different organs of the dense body; the surplusage radiates outwards and energises all living creatures within its range. The very neighbourhood of a vigorously healthy person vitalises, while a weak body draws on all around it for Vitality, often seriously depleting those near to it. Physical magnetism, the power of healing, etc., are ways in which this surplus Vitality may be usefully expended.

Etheric vision—physical vision keener than the normal —may be used for examining minute objects, such as chemical atoms, or the wave-forms of electrical and other forces, or for studying such of the nature-spirits as use etheric matter for their lowest bodies—fairies, gnomes, brownies, and creatures of that ilk. Very slightly increased tenseness of the nerves, caused by excitement, ill-health, drugs, alcohol, may bring these within sight.

The etheric part of the brain plays an active part in dreams, especially in those caused by impressions from outside, or from any internal pressure from the cerebral vessels. Its dreams are usually dramatic, and may embroider any memory of past events, objects, or persons.[1]

In normal healthy persons the etheric part of the physical body does not separate from the dense, but the greater part of it may be driven out by anæsthetics, and slips out easily in the case of persons who are mediumistic, often serving as the basis for materialisations. Death is its complete withdrawal from its dense counterpart, in conjunction with the consciousness in the higher bodies; it remains with these for a varying interval—usually about thirty-six hours after death—and then is thrown off by the Man as of no further use; it decays away *pari passu* with the dense corpse.

[1] See the many cases given in Du Prel's *Philosophy of Mysticism.*

THE EMOTIONAL OR ASTRAL SPHERE, ITS WORLDS AND ITS INHABITANTS

The astral sphere connected with our earth contains two globes with which we need not here concern ourselves, also the astral world and its inhabitants, and the intermediate or desire world, a part of the astral, the inhabitants of which are normally under special conditions. The whole sphere belongs to the state of consciousness which shows itself as feelings, desires, and emotions; these changes in consciousness are accompanied with vibrations in astral matter, and as astral matter is fine and very rapid in its vibratory motions, the vibrations are visible to astral sight as colours. The passion of anger causes vibrations that yield a flash of scarlet, while a feeling of devotion or love suffuses the astral body with a blue or rosy hue. Each feeling has its appropriate colour, because each is accompanied by its own invariable set of vibrations.

The human astral body is, of course, composed of astral matter, and, when accompanying the physical body, which it permeates and beyond which it extends, it appears as a cloud, or as a defined oval, according as its owner is little or much developed. Clearness and brightness of the more delicate colours, increased definiteness of form and increase of size mark the higher evolution. When the Man in his higher bodies draws away from the physical—as he does every night in sleep—then the astral body assumes the likeness of the physical. Astral matter being very plastic under the influence of thought, a man appears in the astral world in the likeness of himself, as he sees himself, wearing the clothes of which he thinks. A soldier, slain in battle, and appearing in his astral body to a distant friend, will bear his wounds; a drowned man will appear in dripping clothes. While human beings in the astral world normally wear human forms, the inhabitants of that world who have not had physical bodies—higher fairies, nature-spirits connected with the evolution of plant and animal life, and the like—wear bodies that are constantly changing their outlines and sizes. Sportive elementals—as nature-spirits are often called—will sometimes take advantage of this plasticity of astral matter to swell themselves up into huge and terrible shapes for the sake of terrifying untrained intruders into their world. Some drugs, such as hashish, bhang, opium, and extreme alcoholic poisoning, so affect the physical nerves as to render them susceptible to astral vibrations, and then the patients catch glimpses of some inhabitants of the astral world. The horrors which torment a man suffering from delirium tremens are largely due to the sight of the loathsome elementals that gather round places where liquor is sold, and feed on its exhalations, and are attracted round him by the effluvia of his own drink-sodden body.

All feelings of pleasure and pain in the physical body are due to the presence of the interpenetrating astral, and, if this be driven out by anæsthetics or mesmerism, feeling disappears from the physical body. In sleep—during which the etheric double does not leave its dense counterpart—the astral can be very quickly recalled by any disturbance of the physical body; but where much of the etheric matter has also been driven out, the bridge of communication is broken, and trance is produced; under these conditions the dense body can be seriously mutilated without pain supervening. Pain will, however, show itself as soon as the astral body slips again into the physical, and "consciousness returns". It may be said, in passing, that the normal centre of human consciousness at the present stage of evolution is in the astral body, from which it works on the physical. "Physical consciousness" is now sub-conscious—if such a bull may be permitted to an Irishwoman.

The condition of a person during sleep varies with his stage of evolution. The undeveloped man, in his higher bodies, leaving the physical body, hovers round the places with which he is familiar; the average man drifts towards persons to whom he is attracted, but his attention is turned inwards, and he communes with his friends mentally only; at a stage a little higher, his mind is very active and receptive, and can work out problems presented to it more easily than in the physical body, as witness the common sayings: "sleep brings counsel," "better sleep on it," and the like. A problem quietly placed in the mind on going to sleep will generally be found answered in the morning. All these people do not work consciously in the astral world; for this it is necessary that the attention should be turned outwards, not inwards. Where a man is pure and self-controlled, and shows helpfulness in the physical world, he is often "awakened" in the astral world by a more advanced person. The process consists merely in inducing him to attend to what is going on around him, instead of remaining immersed in thought; his astral body has evolved and has become organised by his mental and moral activities, and he has only to wake up to his astral surroundings. His helper explains matters to him, and for a time keeps him near him; he shows him that astral matter obeys his thought, that he can move at will and at whatever speed he wishes, that he can walk through rocks, dive into seas, pass through raging fires, step over a precipice and hover in air, always provided that he is fearless and confident; if he loses courage, and only then, he is in danger, and the imagined injury may "repercuss," *i.e.* show itself on the physical body as a bruise, a scratch, a wound, etc. When he has learned these preliminary lessons, and can see and hear correctly in the astral world, he is set to work to help the "living" and the "dead"; he is then what we call "an invisible helper," and spends his night in succouring those in trouble, teaching the ignorant, guiding those who have newly arrived in the astral world through the gateway of death. To these last we must now turn.

THE DESIRE WORLD, OR PURGATORY

This is the part of the astral world in which conditions are specialised for discarnate human beings, who, unless they have knowledge, are not free in the astral world, but are " the spirits in prison " spoken of by S. Peter. They are held prisoners by their desires, and hence the name of desire world is given to their abode.

We have seen that, at death, the Man, clothed in his finer bodies, draws himself out of the physical garment worn during earth-life, the " coat of skin " with which " the first man " was clothed after his " fall " into matter, caused by his seizure of " knowledge ". " Which things are an allegory," as S. Paul says of the story of Abraham, Sarah, and Hagar. Having cast off his coat of skin, the Man is himself, just as he was while clothed with it, and he " goes to his own place " in the astral world, the place for which he has fitted himself. A re-arrangement of the matter of his astral body takes place automatically, unless he has knowledge enough to present it. During the life of the physical body, the astral particles from all the seven astral subdivisions of matter move freely about among themselves, and some of all kinds are always on the surface of the astral body; sight of the whole astral world depends on the presence on the surface of the astral body of particles drawn from all the seven subdivisions, which answer to our solids, liquids, gases, and the four states of ether. These particles are not gathered together and fashioned into an organ of vision, like the physical eye; when the Man turns his attention outwards he sees " all over him," through all these particles, or through such of them as are in the direction of the object towards which his attention is turned.[1] If the rearrangement of the

[1] New-comers in the astral world always look through the astral simulacra of eyes, because accustomed to turn their attention outwards in that way, just as they move their legs for walking. Both are unnecessary.

matter of the astral body takes place, the matter of each subdivision is gathered together, and a series of concentric shells is formed, the densest being outside. Hence the Man can only see the subdivision of the astral world to which the outermost shell belongs; the amount of each kind of matter depends on the kind of desires and emotions he has cultivated on earth. If these have been of a low order, the densest astral matter will be very strongly vitalised, and this outermost shell, placing him in touch with the lowest division of the astral world only, will last for a long time; it disintegrates by slow starvation, *i.e.* by the deprivation of its accustomed satisfactions. Hence a drunkard, a glutton, a sensualist, a man of violent and brutal passions, having strongly vitalised by physical indulgence the densest and coarsest combinations of astral matter, can only be conscious of his surroundings through these, and sees only people like himself, and the worst qualities of those who are of better types; his raging passions can find no satisfaction, because he has lost the physical organs by which he erstwhile gratified them; moreover, these passions are much more violent than before, for during his physical life most of the force of the astral vibrations was used up in merely setting in motion the heavy physical particles of matter, and only what was left over was felt as pleasure or pain; hence all passions are pale and weak on earth compared with their violence in the astral world, where, after easily setting in motion the light astral particles, they show the whole remainder of their force as pleasure or pain, as a rapture or an agony inconceivable on earth. This last is what religions call "hell"—and a veritable hell, as to suffering, it is, created by the man for his own dwelling-place. But it is only temporary, and might more fitly therefore, for orthodox Christians and Musalmāns, be called "purgatory".[1] The thick layer of densest matter

[1] Both these religions, while ordinarily speaking of hell as everlasting, have passages in their Scriptures which contradict the

wears away, and the man loses sight of this sphere of astral life and begins to perceive the next, having learned, by the sad lesson of bitter suffering, that the pleasures he valued on earth are verily "wombs of pain".

The average man does not experience this unfortunate after-death condition, not having drawn into his astral body while on earth much of the densest matter, and such of it as he has is not strongly vitalised, and it cannot hold him. If his interests on earth have all been trivial—a round of office or household drudgery or manual labour, alternating with low, though not vicious, forms of amusement—and he has cared nothing for larger interests, those of the community and the nation, he will find himself shelled in by matter of the sixth subdivision of the astral world, and will be surrounded by the astral counterparts of physical objects, without the power to affect them or to take part in the earth-life led among them; he will, therefore, to use a colloquialism, find himself very much bored, and be a prey to an intolerable sense of ennui. It may be said that this is hard, as most people have to spend their lives in drudgery of some kind; are they to be bored after death, having drudged before it? True; but a little knowledge will prevent this, and for this very reason Theosophy is being spread far and wide. The work which carries on the world need not be drudgery, and to deeply religious people is not drudgery even now; for all useful work is part of the divine Activity, and all workers are organs of that Activity, the Hands wherewith the divine Worker accomplishes His work. Production and distribution—agriculture, mining, manufactures, commerce, the pettiest trade—are God's ways of nourishing humanity, and are the means of evolution. When a man, a woman, see their little daily tasks as integral portions of the one great work, they are no longer

idea. The New Testament speaks of a time when "God shall be all in all," and Al Qurān declares: "All things shall perish save His Face."

drudges but co-workers with God.[1] As George Herbert sang:

> "A servant in this cause
> Makes drudgery divine;
> Who sweeps a room as for Thy laws
> Makes that and th' action fine."

Those who thus work will find no boredom after death, but fresh and joyous activity. For the rest, they gradually adapt themselves to the new conditions, and are helped to do so, and they find that they are rid of many of the discomforts of earth, and may lead a quite pleasant life; they are in touch with their friends on earth, and find that these are quite companionable during earth's nights, though provokingly indifferent during its days; as Mr. Leadbeater pithily says: "The dead are never for a moment under the impression that they have lost the living," however much the latter lament the loss of the dead they loved. The man passes on through the sixth, fifth, and fourth subdivisions, enjoying more and more association with those he loves, until he passes into the higher subdivisions—the material heavens of the less instructed religionists of all faiths, the region for art, literature, science, philanthropy, and the large interests of life, followed on earth with some selfishness, and here pursued along the habitual physical lines and with the use of astral reproductions of physical means and apparatus. These same pursuits, carried on for unselfish motives, lift the Man into the heaven-world, their proper home, and thither also those who followed them more selfishly pass, for when they weary of them in the astral world they fall asleep, to wake in heaven.

The astral body has been cast off, shell after shell, and in due time goes back to its elements, like the physical. Some pure and lofty souls pass through the astral world without attending to it, their minds set upon higher things. Others, fully awake, do not allow the

[1] See *Application of Theosophy to Social Problems*, Section V., p. 77.

matter of their astral bodies to be rearranged, but retain their freedom and perform useful service. Omitting this last class, whose stay in the astral world will depend on other causes, the general rule is that the astral after-death life is long for the undeveloped and short for the well-developed, while the heavenly is long for the latter and short for the former.

THE MENTAL SPHERE, ITS WORLDS AND ITS INHABITANTS

The mental sphere connected with our earth contains two globes with which we are not now concerned. It contains also two worlds, the higher and the lower, each with its inhabitants, and a part of the lower is placed under special conditions, for the use of discarnate human beings; this is the heaven-world. The whole sphere belongs to the state of consciousness denominated thought, or mental activity, and its matter answers to the changes in consciousness that are caused by thinking; its seven subdivisions, though so much finer, again correspond to those of the physical and astral worlds. And the mental world is, like the physical, divided into two, a lower and an upper, the former consisting of the four denser sub-divisions and the latter of the three subtler; two bodies belong to it: the mental, composed of combinations of the denser, and the causal, composed of those of the finer. This world is of peculiar interest, not only because Man spends here nearly all his time, after the mind is fairly developed, only dipping down into the physical world for brief snatches of mortal life as a bird dives into the sea after a fish, but because it is the meeting-place of the higher and the lower consciousnesses. The immortal Individuality, descending from above—after the Monad has formed the Spirit by sending out his ray—waits in high heaven, while the lower bodies are being formed round the atoms attached to him, brooding over them through long ages of slow evolution; when they are sufficiently evolved, he flashes down and takes possession of them, to use them for his own evolution. The habitat of the Spirit as Intellect—of him "whose nature is knowledge"—is the causal world, the three higher levels of the mental sphere; these give him his body, the causal, the body which remains, ever evolving, throughout his long series of incarnations in denser matter. This world and body are so named because all the causes, the effects of which are seen in the lower worlds, reside in them. The causal body begins, with the above-named flashing down, as a mere film of matter, egg-shaped, like a shell round the lower bodies, formed within it, as the chick in the egg. A delicate network radiates from the permanent atom of the causal body to all parts of this egg-like film, the atom glowing like a brilliant nucleus; with it are associated the permanent atoms of the physical and astral bodies and the permanent molecule-unit of the mental. During life, it encloses the whole bodies, and at the death of each it preserves this permanent germ of each, with all the vibratory powers enshrined within it, the "seed of life" for each successive body. For ages it is little more than this subtle network and surface, for it can only grow by the higher human activities, by such as arouse in its subtle matter a faint vibratory response; as the personality grows more thoughtful, more unselfish, more engaged in right activities, its harvest for its owner grows richer and richer. The personalities are like the leaves put forth by a tree; they draw in material from outside, transform it into useful substances, send it down the tree as crude sap, drop off and wither; the sap is changed into tree-food, and nourishes the tree, which sends out new leaves, to repeat the same cycle. The consciousness, in the mental, astral, and physical bodies, gathers experience; casting off the physical and astral bodies, as dead leaves, it transmutes these experiences into qualities in the mental body, during its heavenly life; it is indrawn into the causal body with its harvest, casting away the mental body, like the others, and is blended with the Spirit, who put it forth, enriching him with its harvest; it has served the Spirit as a hand, put forth to take food. The enriched Spirit, the Man, forms, round the old permanent atoms, another mental and astral body, capable of manifesting his enhanced qualities; the physical permanent atom is planted through the father in the body of the mother who is to provide the physical body required by the changeless law of cause and effect, and these three lower bodies are nourished and coloured by her corresponding bodies; the new personality is thus launched into the mortal world.[1]

While Intellect has, as its vehicle, the causal body, its copy in denser matter, the Mind, has the mental body as its instrument; the one has abstract thinking as its activity, the other concrete. The Mind acquires knowledge by utilising the senses for observations, its percepts, and by working on these and building them into concepts; its powers are attention, memory, reasoning by induction and deduction, imagination, and the like. The Intellect *knows*, by the assonance of the outside world with its own nature, and its power is Creation, the arrangement of matter into bodies for its own natural products, Ideas. When it sends a flash into the lower Mind, illuminating its concepts and inspiring its imagination, we call the flash Genius.

Both the causal and mental bodies expand enormously in the later stages of evolution, and manifest the most gorgeous radiance of many-coloured lights, glowing with intense splendour when comparatively at rest, and sending forth the most dazzling coruscations when in high activity. Both interpenetrate the lower bodies and extend beyond their surface, as has already been stated with regard to the etheric double and the astral body. The parts of all these bodies of finer matter which are outside the dense physical body form collectively the "aura" of the human being, the luminous coloured cloud surrounding his dense body. The etheric portion of the aura can be seen by Dr. Kilner's

[1] The reader is advised to refer to the table on p. 25.

apparatus; an ordinary clairvoyant usually sees this and the astral portion; a clairvoyant more highly developed sees the etheric, astral, and mental portions. Few are able to see the portion consisting of the causal body, and fewer still the rare beauty of the intuitional, and the dazzling light of the spiritual, vehicles.

The clarity, delicacy, and brilliance of the auric colours, or their opacity, coarseness, and dullness, show the general stage of advancement of the owner. Changes of emotion suffuse the astral portion with transitory colours, as with the rose of love, the blue of devotion, the grey of fear, the brown of brutality, the sickly green of jealousy. The pure yellow of intelligence, the orange of pride, the brilliant green of mental sympathy and alertness, are equally familiar. Striations, bands, streaks, flashes, etc., give a multiplicity of forms for study, all expressive of certain qualities in the mental and moral character. The child's aura, again, differs much from that of the adult. But we must pass on, as space is limited.

The Mind, working in the mental body, produces results—thoughts—in the astral and physical bodies, in the latter by using as its instrument the cerebro-spinal system. In its own world it sends out definite "thought-forms," thoughts embodied in mental matter, which go forth into the mental world and may incorporate themselves in other mental bodies; its own vibrations, also, send out undulations in all directions, that cause similar vibrations in others. Comparatively few people, at the present stage of evolution, can function freely in the mental world, clothed only in the higher and the mental bodies, separated from the physical and astral. But those who can do so can tell about its phenomena—an important matter, since heaven[1] is a part of the mental world, guarded from all unpleasant intrusions. The inhabitants of the world are the higher ranks of nature-spirits, called in the East Devas, or Shining Ones, and by Christians, Hebrews, and Muhammadans

[1] Called in the older Theosophical books Devachan, or Sukhāvati.

Angels—the lowest Order of the angelic Intelligences. These are glowing forms with changing shades of exquisite colours, whose language is colour, whose motion is melody.

THE HEAVEN-WORLD

The heaven-portion of the mental world is filled with discarnate human beings, who work out into mental and moral powers the good experiences they have garnered in their earthly lives. Here the religious devotee is seen, rapt in adoring contemplation of the Divine Form he loved on earth, for God reveals Himself in any form dear to the human heart; here the musician fills the air with melodious sounds, cultivating his capacity into higher power; here all that love are in close touch with their beloved, and love gains new strength and depth by fullest expression; here the artists of form and colour work out splendid conceptions in plastic material, responsive to their thought; here philanthropists shape great schemes for human helping, architects of plans to be wrought out when they return to earth. Every high activity followed on earth, every noble thought and aspiration, here grow into flowers, flowers which contain within themselves the seeds which shall later be sown on earth. Knowing this, men may in this world prepare the seeds of experience which shall flower in heaven. The cultivation of every literary and artistic faculty, of patient and steadfast love, of unselfish service to man, of devotion to God, make a full and rich and fruitful heaven. Those who sow sparingly reap sparingly; while everyone's cup of happiness will be filled to overflowing, we make our cups large or small here. The length of our heaven depends on the materials we can carry through death, and these materials are good thoughts and pure emotions. It may stretch to fifteen hundred or two thousand years; it may be but a few centuries; in the very little developed even less.

When the whole of the experience has been worked

up into faculty, the Man casts off his mental body, and is then truly himself, living in the causal and the two higher bodies. If highly developed, he may live awhile in the higher levels of the mental worlds; generally his stay there is very brief, only sufficient to allow him to see his whole past and to glance over his coming life, and he quickly begins to put himself down again, driven by hunger for more experience. The germs of the developed mental faculties are planted in mental matter, to form a new mental body; those of the developed emotional and moral faculties in astral matter, to form a new astral body, and these are the "innate faculties," the "character," which a child brings with him into the world.

THE HIGHER SPHERES

The two higher spheres, the intuitional, in which the Christ-nature unfolds in the Man, and the spiritual, cannot be here fully described. The Intuition, the clear insight into the nature of things—that sees the one Self in all and destroys the sense of separateness—is the faculty of the Wisdom-nature, the supreme spiritual *vision*, for which "Nature has no veil in all her kingdoms". The spiritual sphere, in which the unity of the human will with the divine is realised, is the last and highest in the at present manifested system—the monadic and the divine spheres being, as yet, unmanifested. The wheel of normal human evolution revolves in three worlds—the physical, the intermediate, and the heavenly: in the first we gather experience; in the second we suffer and enjoy according to our life in the first; in the third we enjoy unalloyed happiness, and transmute experience into faculty, past suffering into power. These we bring back, and thus we grow and evolve, age after age.

Each stage of this æonian evolution may be studied by quickening the unfolding of the consciousness, and the growth of the bodies belonging to the different worlds. No statement made in this Section need be taken on trust—save that about the Monad—but the study which enables verification to be fully made is as arduous as that of the highest mathematics or astronomy. A slight development beyond the normal will, however, enable etheric and astral facts to be examined, and such experience may encourage the student to pursue the further task.

RELIGIOUS CEREMONIES AND RITES

A great service rendered by Theosophy as Science to the various religions is the explanation it offers of their several ceremonies and rites. These were originally planned out by great Occultists in order to convey to the devoted and the good the influences of the higher spheres. A "sacrament" is well defined in the Catechism of the Church of England as "the outward and visible sign of an inward and spiritual grace," and it is not only a sign that the grace is present, but a means whereby it may be conveyed to the worshipper. By the old rules there must be for a sacrament an outer physical Object, a Sign of Power, and a Word of Power, and there must also be an Officiant duly qualified according to the laws of the religion. Thus, in Christian Baptism, Water is the physical Object, the Sign of Power is the Cross, the Word of Power is the baptismal formula: "I baptize thee in the Name of the Father, and of the Son, and of the Holy Ghost"; the Officiant is the duly ordained minister. The inward spiritual grace is the blessing poured out on the child by the surrounding Angels, his admission to the community of Christians in this and other worlds, and the welcome extended to him by the invisible and visible Christian Church. In the Holy Communion the same principle is followed, and any clairvoyant, watching the ceremony, will see a blazing out of light, following the words of consecration, the light flashing out through the church and bathing the worshipper, and being appropriated and drawn in by the really devoted; it is because of the tradition of this "real Presence" that the Host is preserved in Roman Catholic churches, and from it, as a matter of fact, radiates a constant blessing. Ceremonies performed to help those who have passed on, the so-called "dead," are all based on a knowledge of the facts of the intermediate world, though the persons who take part in them to-day know very little of their real bearing on the one for whom they are done. The daily prayer and meditation, incumbent on every pious Hindū, are intended to draw down and spread abroad gracious spiritual influences, attracting the Devas—"the ministry of Angels"—to shed their blessings on the neighbourhood, on its human, animal, and vegetable lives.

All these things are looked on as "superstitions" by the ordinary, modern man of the world. Yet, since the visible world is interpenetrated and surrounded by the invisible, it is not irrational that the influence of the latter should play on the former. It was regarded as a superstition at the close of the eighteenth century to believe that there was a force which made frogs' legs move when hanging on a wire; Galvani was much laughed at for watching them dance as they awaited the frying-pan, and was called "the frogs' dancing-master". None the less has the galvanic current linked continents together. Many a "superstition" points the way to the discovery of forces unknown to the ordinary man. The wise will observe and investigate, and will study before they reject.

SECTION II

Theosophy as Morality and Art

Morality has been well defined as "the science of harmonious relations"[1] between all living things. Moral laws are as much laws of Nature as are any laws affecting physical phenomena, are to be sought in the same laborious way, and established by the same methods. As physical hygiene was laid down by ancient legislators as part of religion,[2] so did they lay down moral hygiene; both have been accepted as part of "revelation" by their followers, but both are based on the facts of Nature known to these highly developed men, though not to their people.

THE LIFE-SIDE—MORALITY

We have seen that the teaching of one omnipresent Life is part of Theosophy; on this Morality is based. To injure another is to injure yourself, for each is part of a single whole. The body as a whole is poisoned, if poison be introduced into any part of it, and all living things are harmed by harm which is done to one. This one Life expresses itself in everything by seeking for Happiness; everywhere and always, without exception, Life seeks Happiness, and no suffering is ever voluntarily borne except as a road to a deeper and more lasting joy. None seeks aimless suffering, for the mere sake of suffering; it is endured only as means to an end. All religions recognise God as infinite Bliss, and

[1] *Sanātana Dharma Text-Book*, Part III.: Ethics.
[2] As in the laws of Manu and of Moses.

union with God, *i.e.* with perfect Bliss, is sought by all of them. Man's nature, since he is divine, is also fundamentally blissful, and he therefore accepts all happiness as natural, and its coming to him is taken as needing no justification; he never asks: "Why do I enjoy?" But his nature revolts against pain as unnatural, and as needing justification, and he instinctively demands: "Why do I suffer?" Deep, unalloyed, enduring Bliss is the goal of Life; the perfect satisfaction of every part of the being. The fleeting will-o'-the-wisp of earthly pleasure is often mistaken for the glow of the Sun of Bliss, and then man suffers—and learns. "For God has a plan, and that plan is evolution."[1] If the part sets itself against the whole, it must suffer, and all the sufferings of men are due to their ignorance of their own nature, and to their disregard, also due to ignorance, of the laws of the Nature in the midst of which they live.

RIGHT AND WRONG

If evolution is God's plan, then we can gain a definite criterion of Right and Wrong. The scientist will say: That which helps forward evolution is Right; that which hinders it is Wrong. The religionist will say: That which is according to the divine Will is Right; that which is against it is Wrong. Both are expressing exactly the same idea, for the divine Will is evolution. By studying evolution we find that its first half has been developing an ever greater and greater separation—the aim has been the production of the Individual; we find that now, beginning the second half, we are moving towards the integration of individuals into a Unity. The Hindūs call these processes the Path of Forthgoing and the Path of Return, and there are no more expressive names. Man's deepest instincts, showing themselves in the foremost of his race—and instinct

[1] *At the Feet of the Master*, by J. Krishnamurti (Alcyone) p. 7.

is the Voice of Life—are now seeking for Brotherhood, beyond which lies Unity, the building of many parts into a perfect whole. Hence all that makes for unity is Right; all that makes against it is Wrong.

EMOTIONS AND VIRTUES

The next step is that Happiness is essentially a *feeling;* it is due to a sense of the increase of life in us; we are happy when our life expands, when it becomes more; we suffer when our life diminishes, when it becomes less.[1] Love brings about union, and thus moreness; hate causes separation, and hence lessness. We have here the two Root Emotions, Love and Hate, both expressions of Desire—the manifestation of the aspect of Will—which is seen throughout the manifested worlds as Attraction and Repulsion, the Builder and the Destroyer of universes, systems, and worlds, as well as of states, families, and individuals. Out of these two Root Emotions spring all Virtues and Vices; every Virtue is an expression of Love, universalised, and established by right reason as a permanent mode of consciousness; every Vice is an expression of Hate, universalised, and established by wrong reason as a permanent mode of consciousness; "right" and "wrong" have already been defined. This will at once be understood by an illustration drawn from the family, and we may premise that each of us, in Society as in the family, is surrounded by three, and only three, classes —his superiors, his equals, his inferiors, with each of which he has relations. In a happy family, Love unites all the members; Love, looking upwards to the heads of the household, is the emotion of reverence; Love, looking round the circle of brothers and sisters, is the emotion of affection; Love, looking downwards on the group of dependents, is the emotion of beneficence.

[1] On the whole of this subject there is no better book than *The Science of the Emotions*, by Bhagavān Dās, a well-known Theosophical writer.

These emotions spring up spontaneously in the "good" family, the family where "right" feeling rules, and "love is the fulfilling of the law". Where love rules, laws are not needed. Outside the family, when men enter into relations with the general public, the attitude taken spontaneously in the family by Love must be reproduced outside deliberately by Virtue. Looking upwards—as to God, the King, the Aged—the emotion of Love as reverence becomes the Virtues of Reverence, Obedience, Loyalty, Respect, and the like, all fixed attitudes of mind, or permanent modes of consciousness, towards the persons, whoever they may be, who are recognised as superiors, spiritually, intellectually, morally, socially, physically. Looking around on our equals, the emotion of Love as affection becomes the Virtues of Honour, Courtesy, Fairness, Friendliness, Helpfulness, and the like, fixed attitudes of mind towards all, as before. To our inferiors, the emotion of Love as beneficence becomes the Virtues of Protection, Kindness, Courtesy, Readiness to assist, to share with, and the like. The principle once grasped, the student can work out its myriad applications; Hate, with its three main divisions of Fear, Pride, and Scorn, may be similarly treated.

Every human being, living in Society, is related inevitably, by the mere fact of his being there, to all around him, and this makes him the centre of a web of obligations, of duties; to give to each related person his due is to be a "good" man, and a source of social unity; to refuse to any his due is to be a "bad" man, and a source of social disunity. Hence to know Duty and to do it is goodness; to know it intuitively and to do it spontaneously is perfection.

While Life showing itself emotionally is Love, seen intellectually it is Truth. For lack of understanding this, controversies have arisen as to whether Love or Truth should be the foundation of Morality. But they are one essentially, as Life is one. Bhīṣhma, a Master of Duty, said that virtues are "forms of Truth," and that is indubitably so; Truth is the very basis of intellectual character, as is Love of moral character; as Love demands the presence of others for its expression while Truth does not, it naturally rules the science of our harmonious relations with others, and thus flowers into virtues. "God is Love," says the Christian; "Brahman is Truth," says the Hindū. Both speak the fact; seen from below, Love and Truth may look different; seen from above, they are one.

THE RATIONALE OF MORAL PRECEPTS

The great Teachers of humanity have formulated certain universal ethical precepts, such as: "To do good to another is right; to injure another is wrong." "Do to others as you would that they should do to you; do not to others as you would not that they should do to you." "Love one another." "What doth the Lord thy God require of thee, but to do justly, and to love mercy, and to walk humbly with thy God?"[1] All moral teachings inspired by this spirit are parts of the Divine Wisdom, of Theosophy. They need no justification to the mind, for they obviously tend to promote Happiness.

But much light is thrown on the rationale of less obvious precepts by Theosophy; thus to return good for evil is not, at first glance, reasonable. "How then will you recompense good?" asked Confucius. But it is right. We have seen that changes in consciousness are accompanied by vibrations of matter, and that such vibrations are sympathetically reproduced by neighbouring bodies. If a man is feeling angry, or depressed, or revengeful, his astral body will vibrate in assonance with his mood. The astral body of anyone coming near him will be impinged on by these vibrations, and will begin to vibrate in unison with them, these vibrations then producing in the second person a feeling of anger, or depression, or revenge, as the case may be. He will

[1] A large number of extracts from the Scriptures of great religions may be found in the *Universal Text-Book of Religion and Morals*, Part II.

thus strengthen the vibrations produced in his astral body and will return them reinforced, strengthening those of the first, and this fatal interchange will go on, increasing the evil. But if the second person, understanding the law, grips his astral body with his will, prevents it from reproducing the vibrations which strike on it, and imposes on it a contrary set of vibrations, those which accompany a feeling of gentleness, cheerfulness, or forgiveness, he will quiet down the vibrations caused by evil emotion, and presently change them to their opposite. Therefore the Lord Buddha taught: "Hatred ceaseth not by hatred at any time; hatred ceaseth by love." This is as certain as that a red ray of light will quench a green ray, and leave stillness—absence of light vibrations. It is a law of Nature, and one that can readily be verified by experiment. To follow this law is to substitute a harmonious relation for an inharmonious, *i.e.* to be moral.

Theosophy asserts as an ethical code the universal precepts of the great Teachers, and studies their rationale scientifically, as above, and historically, in their effects on human evolution and human happiness. It sees their verification in the disasters that follow the neglect of these precepts, as much as in the security and comfort which follow their observance, even though that observance has never been more than partial, except in the example set by the great Teachers Themselves. Its morality is therefore eclectic; in the garden of the world it culls the fairest and most fragrant flowers, planted by the great Teachers, and binding these into one exquisite bouquet, it names it "Theosophy as Morality".

IDEALS

In order to inspire moral conduct in Theosophists, it points to the great Teachers as Examples, and inculcates the forming of a moral Ideal and the practice of meditation thereon. An ideal is a synthesis of true fixed ideas, intended to be an object of attentive and sustained thought, and thus to influence conduct. By the laws of thought—to be treated in Section III.—the effect of such thought is to transform the thinker into the likeness of his ideal, and thus to build up a noble character. Along this line of moral evolution Theosophists seek to guide all aspirants, trusting "not to the law of a carnal commandment, but to the power of an endless life". We fix our gaze on the World-Teachers, and seek so to live that some ray of Their moral splendour may take embodiment in us, and that we also may, in our humble measure, lighten the darkness of the world.

THE FORM-SIDE—ART

In the older world the Beautiful was placed on a level with the Good and the True, and the cult of Beauty made fair the common lives of men. Pythagoras spoke of the Arts as making "the difference between the barbarian and the man," [1] and Art and pure Literature are the means of culture; they polish the stone, after Science and Philosophy have hewn the rough product of the quarry into shape. Further East than Greece, Beauty held a similar place in civilisation, as it did also in Egypt and in the great Atlantean civilisations in the Americas. In fact no civilisation that the world has ever known, until that of the nineteenth century, has set the Beautiful aside as a luxury for the wealthy, instead of spreading it far and wide over the whole mass of the population as one of the ordinary necessities for decent human life. In nearly every European country the arts and crafts of the peasantry are almost killed out; their old dress, suitable and comely, is being disused, and replaced by miserable copies of grotesque fashions set in Paris and London. The result is that the manual labouring class has been entirely vulgarised, has lost its inborn sense of Beauty—to which its crafts taken up for pastime in leisure hours in the past so eloquently testify—and, in the losing, has become piteously coarse and ill-mannered. The spread of civilised ugliness is threatening the Beauty which still

[1] See Section V., p. 74.

remains to the world in the common life of the further East, and the destructive change may be summed up in a single fact, that the disused kerosene oil-tin is taking the place of the admirably wrought brass or clay vessel for bringing water from the well to the house. When the village girl, who now carries this tin atrocity on her head, drops her graceful sāri with its exquisite vegetable dye, and puts on the ugly aniline-dyed skirt and blouse of the West, she will have completed her own vulgarisation, and the triumph of western civilisation.

BEAUTY AS THE LAW OF MANIFESTATION

From the standpoint of Theosophy, the sense of the Beautiful is a priceless part of the emotional nature, and is to it what Truth is to the Intellect and Goodness to the Intuition. It sees Beauty as the Law of Manifestation, to which all objects should conform. Ugliness is against Nature, unnatural, intolerable. Nature is ever striving to hide it away in order to transform it. She covers all that is ugly with her wealth of Beauty; over a disused slag-heap she trails her creepers; a broken wall she festoons with her honeysuckle-bines, and tosses over it a wreath of pink-faced roses; she plants the wayside ditch with fragrant violets, and draws a sheet of anemones and wild hyacinths over the neglected spaces of the woods. With her myriad voices she preaches that Beauty is the essential condition of divine, and therefore of all perfect, work.

Religion has ever been the foster-mother of Art; the Egyptian faith gave Philæ to the world;[1] Hindūism gave the mighty fanes of Madura and Chidambaran; Greece gave the Parthenon and many another gem; Islām gave the Alhambra, the Pearl Mosque, and the Tāj Mahal; Christianity the noble Gothic cathedrals—to say nothing of the music, painting, sculpture, oratory, that have glorified the life of man. Art is unthinkable without Religion; the most exquisite architecture has been devised for temples, and on them

[1] Modern civilisation has drowned it!

other buildings have been modelled. If it has decayed, it is because Religion has passed so much out of ordinary life, and with the lack of its inspiration Art has become imitative instead of creative. The new Theosophic impulse will bring about a new blossoming of Art, and already its fragrance is borne on the breeze blowing from the future.

CREATION, NOT IMITATION

Imitation, however perfect and enjoyable, is not the highest Art, from the Theosophical standpoint. Forms are built by nature-spirits and lower Angels out of the matter penetrated with the Life of the LOGOS; they built round His thought-forms, materialising His ideas. Looking at an exquisite flower, we, who are human, can see a little more of the divine thought in it than the less developed nature-spirit could see and embody. But the Artist—he can see far more than we; he sees the many-sided thought of which the flower-form is only a facet; he sees the ideal, and it is *that* which we ask him to show us. Rafaelle painted a woman with a child in her arms; we have seen many women carrying their infant sons. But the painter of the San Sisto Madonna saw the ideal Mother and the ideal Child, infinite tenderness and protection in the Mother, exquisite sweetness and candid simplicity in the Child. He saw not only mother and child, but Motherhood and Childhood, the eternal perfection of the Idea, and he painted it for the wonder and the love of every succeeding generation. And we blind ones can now see the Madonna and the Babe in every mother and child, and the whole world is fairer because Rafaelle lived and saw.

Unless Theosophy can give a new inspiration to Art, it will have failed in part of its purpose; for Beauty is one of the most potent instruments for quickening evolution, and harmony, without which life cannot be happy, finds its natural expression in Art. Perfection in form must accompany Perfection in thought.

SECTION III

THEOSOPHY AS PHILOSOPHY

PHILOSOPHY is an explanation of Life, constructed by the Mind and accepted as true by the Intellect. Without an explanation which satisfies the reason, a man remains restless and discontented. The unintelligibility of life is torture to the thoughtful; one cannot rest in the midst of a whirl of forces and of events, a seething chaos, which throws up fragments which cannot be fitted into a rational whole. The Mind imperatively demands order, succession, causal connections, the stately rhythm of purposeful movements, the relation of past to present, of present to future. To understand is the deepest instinct in the Mind of Man, and it can never rest satisfied until this understanding is obtained. Man can suffer patiently, struggle perseveringly, endure heroically, if he feels within him a purpose, sees before him a goal. But if he cannot see his way, does not know his end, is baffled by causes he does not understand, and buffeted by forces which whirl out at him from darkness, strike him, and then whirl into darkness once more, he is apt to break out into wild revolt, into savage rebellion, and to waste his strength in aimless blows. Ajax, fighting in the dark with his frantic appeal to the Gods:

> "If our fate be death,
> Give light, and let us die,"

is a symbol of humanity, struggling in the night of ignorance and passionately crying out to "whatever Gods there be" to send him light, even though light mean death.

THREE BASES FOR PHILOSOPHY

Men have striven to understand the mysteries of existence by approaching them from one of three mutually opposed view-points:

(1) All comes forth from Matter, the One Existence, and this, from its own inherent energy, produces all forms, and gives birth through them to life; as Professor Tyndall said in his famous Belfast address, we must "see in matter the promise and potency of every form of life". Thought is the result of the activity of certain arrangements of matter: "The brain produces thought," said Karl Vogt, "as the liver produces bile". With the dissolution of the form the life vanishes, and it is as idle to ask where "it" is, as to ask where the flame is when the candle burns out. The flame was only the result of combustion, and with the ceasing of combustion the flame necessarily ceases also. All materialistic philosophies are built on this basis.

(2) All comes forth from Spirit, pure mind, the One Existence, and matter is merely a creation of the Spirit engaged in thought. There is really no matter; it is an illusion, and if the Spirit rises above this illusion he is free, self-sufficing, omnipotent. He imagines himself separate, and is separate; he imagines objects, and is surrounded by them; he imagines pain, and he suffers; he imagines pleasure, and he enjoys. Let him sink into himself, and all the universe will fade away as a dream, and "leave not a wrack behind". All idealistic philosophies are built on this basis, with more or less thoroughness in carrying it out.

(3) Spirit and Matter are two aspects of One Existence, the All, coming forth from the One together, united as inseparably during manifestation as the back and front of the same object, merging into Oneness again at the close of a period of manifestation. In the All exist simultaneously all that has been, all that is, all that can be, in one Eternal Present. In this fullness arises a VOICE which is a WORD, a LOGOS, God making

Himself manifest. That WORD separates out, from the All, such Ideas as He selects for His future universe, and arranges them within Himself according to His Will; He limits Himself by His own thought, thus creating the "Ring-Pass-Not" of the universe-to-be—whether Solar System, congery of Solar Systems, congery of congeries, etc. Within this Ring are the Ideas, ever-begotten eternally of the ceaseless Motion, which is the One Life, within the Stillness which is its opposite and supports all. The Motion is the Root of Spirit, which will, when manifest, be Time, or changes in consciousness; the stillness is the Root of Matter, the omnipresent "Æther," immobile, all-sustaining, all-pervading, which will, when manifest, be Space. All Theosophic philosophies are built on this basis, Spirit and Matter being regarded as two manifested aspects of the One, the Absolute, out of Time and Space.[1]

The method of putting these truths will differ much with different thinkers. H. P. Blavatsky has presented them with great force, but with some obscurity of language, in the beginning of *The Secret Doctrine.* Bhagavān Dās makes a singularly profound and lucid statement of them in his *Science of Peace*, where he postulates the Self, the Not-Self—or Spirit and Matter—and the Relation between them, as the great Trinity, the Ultimates of Thought, collapsing into the One.

TRIPLICITY

The LOGOS shows Himself in His universe or system under three aspects—the "Persons" of the Christian Trinity—those of Will, Wisdom (or Knowledge-Love), and Creativeness (or Activity). The human Monad is a fragment of his divine Parent, and reproduces these three aspects in Himself, manifesting them in Man as Spirit. Hence the human spiritual Will, being part of the one Will, is irresistible Power, when the Spirit realises his unity

[1] See for the further working out of this, Section VI., "A few Details about Systems and Worlds".

with the Logos. Hence to the human spiritual Wisdom nothing in Nature can be veiled. Hence by the human spiritual Creativeness all can be achieved.

It is this last aspect in the human Trinity which can build up all that Wisdom can conceive and that Will can determine. As Intellect in the subtler worlds and as Mind in the lower, it stretches out into the cosmos, to know, to understand. By this, whose "nature is knowledge," Man becomes aware of all which is outside himself, the "Not Self," in the Hindū phrase. We have seen that by the use of bodies Man may know the outer universe, and consciousness may become aware of its environment; beginning—to borrow Myers' terminology —with the knowledge of its own earth, as the planetary consciousness, it may stretch out to a knowledge of its universe, as the cosmic consciousness. The reason demands this as a necessary truth, not because it is testified to by the giants of spiritual genius, but because there are growths in the planetary consciousness which are unintelligible, causeless, and useless unless there is a cosmic consciousness which they adumbrate, and towards which they strive. Religion, Art, unselfish self-sacrificing Love are, as they have been called, bye-products and follies, if we are but gnats of a day, dancing in sunshine, scattered in storm; if we build civilisations with infinite toil and suffering only that they may perish; if all that will be left as blurred record of humanity shall be a frozen planet whirling in space till shattered, the weary purposeless labour to be ever renewed, and its results ever destroyed. To the Theosophic philosophy Man is an eternal spiritual Intelligence, whose root is in God, and his countless activities develop his own inherent powers, which none can annihilate unless he himself casts any away as of no further use to him, and even then they remain in the Eternal Memory. To such a Being, universes are but instructive toys, serving his education, and they may crash into splinters without disturbing his serene equanimity, for they are only means to an end. The universe as a treadmill, grinding out nothing, makes existence a burden, life a perpetual punishment, leaving us not even an Imposer of the burden whose pity we might move, or a Judge to whose clemency we might appeal to mitigate the punishment. Theosophy sees Man as an unfolding Power, going from strength to strength, erring only that he may learn, suffering only that he may grow strong, a radiant, rejoicing, victorious Life, whose "growth and splendour have no limit".

Philosophically considered, Man, like all else, is composed of but two factors, Spirit and Matter. The various bodies which occult Science describes are, from the philosophical view-point, his material sheath. They are, in their totality, merely his Body. Man is a spiritual Intelligence in a Body. The constituents which go to form this Body—physical, emotional, mental, intellectual, intuitional, spiritual forms of matter—are no more germane to the study than are the solids, liquids, gases, and ethers that compose the physical body of man.

THOUGHT-POWER

Thought being the manifestation of Creativeness, the third aspect of the human triplicity, Theosophic philosophy applies it to quicken human evolution. The application of the general laws of the evolution of mind to this quickening of the evolution of a particular consciousness is called in the East *yoga*. The word means "union," and is used to indicate the conscious union of the particular with the universal Self, and all the efforts leading to that consummation. The method of yoga is purely scientific, the knowledge of the laws of mental and intellectual evolution having been gained by observation and established by experiment. It has been proved, and can ever be re-proved, that thought, concentrating itself attentively on any idea, builds that idea into the character of the thinker, and a man may thus create in himself any desirable quality by sustained and attentive thinking—meditation.

The careless play of Thought on undesirable ideas and qualities is an active danger, creating a tendency towards such undesirable things, and leading to actions embodying them. "Action" is a triplicity; desire conceives it, thought plans it, and the final act is the embodiment of both. Hence that final act is often precipitated by favourable circumstances when desire has grown strong, and thought has completely sketched the carrying out; the mental action precedes the physical, and when a man has dallied in thought with the idea of a good or of an evil action, he may find himself performing it in the outer world even before he realises what he is doing; when the gate of opportunity has swung open, the mental action rushes out into the physical.

Concentrated mental activity may be directed to the mental, emotional, and physical bodies, recreating them to an extent proportional to the energy, perseverance, and concentration employed. All schools of healing—Christian Science, Mental Science—utilise this powerful agency in obtaining their results, and their utility depends on the knowledge of the practitioner as to the force which he is employing, and as to the environment in which he is using it—the environment consisting largely of the bodies of his patient. Innumerable successes prove the existence of the force that is wielded, and failures do not show that the force is non-existent, but only that the manipulation of it was not skilful, or could not evoke sufficient of it for the task in hand.

Thought-power being recognised in Theosophic philosophy as the one Creator, it is seen as working in Evolution, and as having planned for the evolution of the human consciousness the admirable method of Reincarnation, under the Law of Action and Reaction, called in the East Karma.

Reincarnation

The object of Man's assumption of bodies—Incarnation—has already been explained; we have seen that his three higher bodies form his permanent clothing, and that they grow and increase with the unfolding of his consciousness. We have seen also that the three lower bodies are temporary, existing through a definite life-cycle, spent by him in three worlds—the earth, the intermediate world, and heaven; with his return to the earth he assumes new bodies, and this is Reincarnation. The necessity for this lies in the comparative density of the matter of which the lower worlds are composed; the bodies made of this can only grow and expand within certain limits, far narrower than those which belong to the subtler bodies; stretched beyond these, by the constant unfolding of consciousness, they lose their elasticity, and can no longer be used; moreover, they grow old by this constant stretching, and wear out. When the consciousness, at the end of a cycle of growth, has definitely established itself in its new stage of evolution, it needs new bodies shaped for the expression of its enhanced powers. If this were not arranged for in the Plan we should be like children enclosed in iron armour, and stunted in their growth by its non-expansiveness. Children "grow out of their clothes," and we give them new ones; we grow out of our bodies, and are given new ones by our Father, the Logos.

The method is simple enough; a seed of divine consciousness is sown in the soil of human life; nourished by that soil, which is experience, stimulated by the sunshine of joy, expanded by the rain of sorrow, it swells and burgeons out into plant, flower, and fruit, until it attains the likeness of the parent tree.

Put without metaphor: a human Spirit, a germinal life, enters the babe of a savage; he has scarcely any intelligence, no moral sense; he lives there for some forty or fifty years, dominated by desires, robs, murders.

finally is murdered. He passes into the intermediate world, meets many old enemies, suffers, sees dimly that his body was murdered as a result of murdering others, comes to a vague conclusion unfavourable to murder; this is very faintly impressed on his consciousness; he enjoys the results of any dawning love he may have felt; he comes back a trifle more "knowledgeable" than at his first birth. This is repeated over and over again, till he has gradually but definitely arrived at conclusions that murder and theft and other such actions cause unhappiness, and love and kindness cause happiness; he has thus acquired a conscience, though there is not much of it, and it is easily overborne by any strong desire. The interval between births is at first very short, but it gradually lengthens, as his thought-power increases, until the regular round of the three worlds is established; in the first he gathers experience; in the second he suffers for his mistakes; in the third he enjoys the outcome of his good thoughts and emotions, and here also he works the whole of his good mental and moral experiences into mental and moral faculties; in this heavenly world, further, he studies his past life, and his sufferings, due to his mistakes, bring him knowledge, and thus power. "Every pain that I suffered in one body became a power which I wielded in the next."[1] His stay in the third world increases in length and richness of yield as he progresses.

At last he approaches the term of his long pilgrimage; he enters the Path, passes through the great Initiations, and reaches human perfection.[2] For him, Reincarnation is over, for he has spiritualised matter for his own use, and while he may wear it, it cannot blind or rule him.

Looking at this long-turning wheel of Births and Deaths, a man may feel a sense of weariness. But it must be remembered that each life-period is new to the one living through it; by a wise arrangement, a man

[1] Edward Carpenter, *Towards Democracy*, "The Struggle of Man with Satan."

[2] See Section IV., "The Path to Perfection and Divine Men."

down here forgets his past, at least until he is strong enough to bear its weight, and as Goethe said rejoicingly, we "return bathed" and fresh. There is no sense of weariness in the child, joyously springing out to meet his new life, but a sense of glad vitality, of eager enjoyment, of ever-fresh delights. A wayworn soul, entering into a child's body, weighed down by the memory of past struggles and blunders, of love and hates, would be a poor exchange for the gladness of healthy childhood. Every life is a new opportunity, and if we have wasted one life, we have always "another chance". Reincarnation is essentially a Gospel, good news, for it makes an end of despair, encourages effort, cheers with the proclamation of final success, and ensures the permanence of every fragment, every seed, of good in us, and time enough for the least evolved to flower into perfection.

Its value as an explanation of life is untold. The criminal, the lowest and vilest, the poorest, foulest specimen of our race, is only a baby-soul, coming into a savage body, and thrown into a civilisation for which he is unfit if left to follow his own instincts, but which will provide for him a field of rapid evolution if his elders take him in hand and guide him firmly and gently. He is now at the stage at which the average commonplace men were standing a million or so years ago, and he will evolve in the future as they have evolved in the past. There is no partiality shown to those who are situated differently from him; there is only difference of age. The *inborn inequality* in men need no longer distress us—the inequality between the splendidly shaped and the cripple, the healthy and the diseased, the genius and the fool, the saint and the criminal, the hero and the coward. True, they are born thus, and bring with them into the world these inequalities which they cannot transcend. But they are either much younger in experience, or have built themselves as they are under the laws of nature; every weakness will disappear in time, opportunity after opportunity will come to them, every height is open to them to climb with the strength necessary for its scaling.

The knowledge of Reincarnation guides us, as we shall see in Section V., in dealing with social problems. It shows us also how the social instincts have evolved, why self-sacrifice is the law of evolution for man, how we may plan out our own future evolution under natural laws. It teaches us that qualities evolved from earthly experience are returned to earth for the service of man, and how every effort brings its full result under unerring law. By giving him sufficient time, it puts into man's hands the power to make his destiny as he wills, and to create himself after his ideals. It points to a future of ever-growing power and wisdom, and rationalises our hope of immortality. It makes the body the instrument of the Spirit instead of his owner, and removes the fear that as the Spirit required a physical body in order to come into existence at birth, he is likely to perish when deprived of that body by death. As Hume said, it is the only theory of immortality that the philosopher can look at.

Memory of past lives has its seat in the Intellect not in the Mind, in the permanent individual not in the mortal person. We saw in Section I. that the lower bodies perished at and after death, and that new ones were built wherewith to enter on the new life-period. These have not passed through the experiences of past lives; how, then, should the memory of these abide in them? The man who would remember his past must become conscious in the causal body, wherein the means of memory reside, and learn further to send down the memories garnered therein into his consciousness working in the brain. Through the practice of yoga this may be done, and he can then unroll and read the imperishable scroll of the past.

We are in the habit of regarding Reincarnation from the view-point of the mortal nature of man, and thus seeing a succession of lives, which we describe as "re-incarnations". But it might sometimes be well to consider the question from the view-point of the Eternal Man, the Monad manifesting as the triple Spirit. Thus looked at Reincarnation disappears, unless we say that a tree reincarnates with each spring when it puts out a new crop of leaves, or a man reincarnates when he puts on a new coat. This personality, which looms so large down here, is only a new set of leaves, or a new coat. The Man knows *himself* as one Man all through, with an unbroken continuity of consciousness, with a single identity, and an uninterrupted memory. The days of his mortal life have for him no more weariness than the long succession of mortal days have for our consciousness working in the physical body; we rise in the morning and go forth to interests ever renewed, and each new day brings its own pleasures and pains which we live through with zest. The fact that our physical body is always changing does not trouble us a bit; *we* are the same, inside it. And so, in the larger life, *we* are the same, the ever-living, ever-working Spirits. When we realise this, pain and weariness drop away, for we see them as belonging to that which is not ourselves. To stand in the fixed centre, and to look at the whirling wheel from there, is very refreshing and very useful. If any of my readers feel tired, I would invite them to seek for awhile this Place of Peace.

THE LAW OF ACTION AND REACTION

Reincarnation is carried on under the Law of Action and Reaction—Karma. The word karma means action, and we have seen above that every action is a triplicity. The Hindū, who has studied psychology for thousands of years, analyses action as made up of three factors: thought, stimulated by desire, plans out and shapes it; will (or desire) draws the mental energies together and directs them towards accomplishment; the act itself takes form in the mental world. It is then ready for manifestation, and is, as it were, pressing outwards towards embodiment; it is thrown out into the physical world, when the thinker can create an opportunity by his will-power, or when an opportunity presents itself. It is then precipitated as a visible act. The whole process is regarded by the Hindū as a triple unity, and he calls it "Karma," action. The clear understanding of this is needed for the grasping of the three subsidiary laws which affect our future destiny.

But first it is necessary to realise that karma is a law of nature, and not an arbitrary enactment which may be changed at will, and that it brings about results, but does not reward or punish. A law of nature is not a command, but a relation, an invariable sequence. It does not reward or punish, but yields invariable, and therefore foreseeable, results.

It may be stated generally as follows: Where A and B are in a certain relation to each other, C will follow. Suppose we object to C; we must keep A and B out of that relation. Nature does not say: "You must have C." You must have it, if A and B are in a certain relation to each other; but if you can keep A and B out of that relation by any device—by the interposition of some force, some obstacle—C will not appear. Hence the better we understand Nature, the more can we have our own way in the midst of her laws; every law of Nature is an enabling force to the man of understanding, though a compelling force to the ignorant; we are perfectly free to balance these forces against each other, to neutralise those which are against our purpose while we leave free to act those only which will accomplish it. It was truly said: "Nature is conquered by obedience." The ignorant man is her slave and her plaything; the man of knowledge is her conqueror and her king.

Karma is a Law of Nature; it compels the ignorant, but it gives freedom to the wise. The three subsidiary expressions of it that bear most on our destiny are: "Thought builds character"; "Desire attracts its object, and creates opportunity for grasping it"; "Action causes a favourable or unfavourable environment according as it has brought happiness or unhappiness to others." (1) We have already seen the first, in dealing with thought-power; anyone who chooses to spend five minutes regularly every morning in steady thought on any virtue which he does not possess will find that virtue—after a time the length of which depends on the steadiness and strength of his thought—showing itself forth in his character. (2) A strong and firm wish brings about its own accomplishment; this is very often seen within the limits of a single life; a review of several successive lives places the existence of the law beyond doubt. (3) Those who make others happy, reap happiness for themselves; happiness is found by not seeking it, and ever eludes those who grasp at it most passionately. Most strongly does this, again, come out in reviewing a succession of lives; the man who has caused widespread happiness is born into prosperous circumstances, while the man who has caused unhappiness appears in an unfortunate environment. But so exactly does the law work—"Thought builds character"—that if he has caused the happiness from a selfish motive his selfishness will result in a nature which is itself miserable, even when surrounded by all that should make life pleasant:

> "Though the mills of God grind slowly yet they grind exceeding small;
> Though He stands and waits with patience, with exactness grinds He all."

Karma being the result, at any given time, of all the thoughts, desires, and actions of the past, manifested in our character, our opportunities, and our environment, it limits our present: If we are mentally dull, we cannot suddenly become brilliant; if we have few opportunities, we cannot always create them; if we are crippled, we cannot be hale. But as we created, so can we change it; and our present thoughts, desires, and actions are changing our future Karma day by day. Moreover, it is well to remember, especially if we are facing a coming disaster, that the Karma behind us is as mixed as our present thoughts, desires, and actions. A review of any day will show that it contains some good thoughts and some bad, some noble desires and some base, some kindly actions and some unkindly. Each kind has its full effect, the good making good Karma and the bad making bad. Hence when we face misfortune we have behind us a stream of force which will aid us in turning it aside, and another which weakens us. One of these may be overwhelmingly strong, helping or hindering us; if so, our present effort will play but a small part in the result; but very often the two forces are fairly equally balanced, and a strong present effort will turn the scale. A knowledge of Karma should thus strengthen effort, not paralyse it—as unfortunately is sometimes the case with those whose knowledge is very small. It must never be forgotten that Karma, being a law of Nature, leaves us just as much freedom as we are able to take. To talk of "interfering with Karma" is to talk nonsense, except in the sense that one may talk of interfering with gravitation. In that sense we may interfere with both just as much as we can. If our muscles are weak from fever, we may be unable to walk upstairs against gravitation; but if they are strong, we can run up gaily, defying gravitation to keep us in the hall below. So with Karma. Once more, Nature does not command anyone to do one thing or another; she lays down invariable conditions under which things can, or cannot, be done. It is for us to find out the conditions which will enable us to succeed, and then all her forces work with us and accomplish our desires. "Yoke your waggon on to a star," said Emerson, and then the force of the star will draw your waggon to the place where you would have it.

One other practical point is of grave importance. We may in the past have made some special kārmic force for evil so strong that we are unable to overbear it by any force we can bring to bear against it to-day. Under such circumstances we are driven to do wrong, even when we wish to do right, and we feel ourselves to be as helpless as a straw driven before the wind.

Never mind. We have still resources. When the temptation to evil comes, we may meet it in one of two ways. Feeling that we *must* yield, we may yield supinely, and thus forge another link in the deadly chain of evil habit. But the knower of Karma says: "I have created this hateful weakness by countless yieldings to low desire; I set against it the higher form of desire, my Will, and I refuse to yield." Battling against the temptation, the man is forced surely back, step by step, until he falls over the precipice, and yields in act, though not in Will. To the eye of the world, he has fallen, a helpless victim in a hopeless slavery. To the eye of the knower of Karma, he has, by his gallant struggle, filed away much of the chain that is still round his limbs; a few more such "failures," and the chain will snap, and he will be free. A habit made by many wrong desires cannot be destroyed by one effort of right desire, except in those rare cases in which the God within awakes, and with one touch of the fiery spiritual Will burns up the chains. Such cases of "conversion" are on record, but most men tread a longer path.

The more we understand Karma, the more it becomes a power *in* our hands, instead of a power which binds them. Here, perhaps more than in anything else, "knowledge is power".

SECTION IV

THEOSOPHY AS RELIGION

WE have seen that Spirit, as Man, has three aspects, manifesting himself as Will, Intuition, and Intellect, in the three subtlest bodies. But the word is also used in a narrower sense, denoting the first of the three aspects, that which is manifested in the highest world of our fivefold system—the spiritual, or nirvāṇic, world, where his manifestation is Will, or Power. Often, also, the word is used to denote the two higher aspects by being made to include Intuition, and no objection can be raised to this. The two aspects indeed represent the "spiritual nature" of the human being, as Intellect and Mind represent his Intelligence, the Emotions his Feelings, and the Body his instrument of Action. We have seen that as this diversion marks out the four great departments of human thought—the scientific, the ethico-artistic, the philosophical, and the religious—it is therefore a convenient one. But for the sake of perfect clearness I shall use the word "Spirit" to denote the Monad clothed in an atom of the highest manifested world, and the word "Intuition" to denote him clothed in an additional atom of the next lower one.

The word "Religion" covers Man's search for God and God's answer to the searching. God's answer is His Self-revelation to the seeking Spirit who is Man. As the atmosphere surrounds us and interpenetrates us, but we remain unconscious of its presence though our very life depends on it, so the Universal Spirit surrounds and interpenetrates the particularised Spirit, and the latter knows not Him on whom his life depends:

> "Closer is He than breathing, nearer than hands and feet."

"To know God" is, then, the essence of Religion, as we have seen that all religions testify;[1] all else is subordinate, and the man who thus knows is the Mystic, the Gnostic, the Theosophist. The names are indeed borne by many, but only "those who know" can wear them in their full significance. "God is immanent in everything" is the statement of the truth in Nature which makes such knowledge possible. "God is all and in all" is the Christian way of putting the same truth; though S. Paul puts it in the future, the Mystic puts it in the present. What does it mean?

THE IMMANENCE OF GOD

It means that the essence of Religion is this recognition of God everywhere. The true Theosophist sees in each a portion of the divine Splendour. In the stability of mountains, in the might of crashing billows, in the rush of whirling winds, he sees His Strength. In the star-strewn depths of space, in the wide stretchings of deserts, he sees His Immensity. In the colours of flower-spangled meadows, in the rippling laughter of brooklets, in the green depths of forest shades, in the gleaming expanse of snowy mountain peaks, in the waving of the golden corn in the sunshine, in the silver of wavelets in the moonlight, he sees His Beauty. In the sweet shy smile of the maiden wooed in her dawning, in the eager kiss of the lover who claims her as bride, in the tender eyes of the wife as they rest on the husband, in the answering glance of the husband caressing the wife, in the laughing lips of the child joyous in play, in the warm protecting care of the father and mother, in the steadfast devotion of friend to friend, in the leal fidelity of comrade to comrade, he sees His Love. This is the "recollectedness" of the Mystic, and is the true meaning of the word mistranslated "fear" which "is the beginning of Wisdom". To realise this, and thus to know oneself

[1] See "Introduction".

to be one with God, is the aim of Theosophy, as of all true Religion. All else is means to this end.

THEOSOPHICAL TEACHINGS

The common doctrines of religions, that which has been believed everywhere, at all times, and by everyone, form the body of doctrines promulgated by Theosophy. These are: The One Existence—the One God—manifested in the universe under three Aspects ("Persons," from *persona*, a mask); the hierarchies of superhuman Beings—Devas, Angels, and Archangels; the Incarnation of Spirit in matter, of which Reincarnation is the human phase; the Law of Action and Reaction, "as a man sows, so shall he reap"; the existence of the Path to Perfection, and of divine Men; the three worlds—physical, intermediate, and heavenly—and the higher heavens; the Brotherhood of humanity. These are the leading doctrines of Universal Religion. They can all be proved to be true by the wider Science which investigates the manifested worlds, excluding none from its study so far as its instruments can reach. Hence Theosophy is everywhere the defender and helper of religions, serving each in its own domain, pointing out to each man the sufficiency of his own faith, and urging him to deepen and spiritualise his beliefs rather than to attack the forms preferred by others. It is thus a peacemaker among conflicting creeds, a carrier of goodwill, amity, and tolerance wherever it goes. Knowing that all religions come from one source, the White Brotherhood, it discourages bitterness of feeling among religionists and all virulent attacks by one on another. And hence we say of the Theosophical Society, its vehicle: "Peace is its watchword, as Truth is its aim."

THE PATH TO PERFECTION AND DIVINE MEN

This is a teaching which, though found in all religions, has dropped much out of sight in modern days, till reproclaimed in Theosophy, and may therefore be fitly sketched here. It is very fully described in Hindūism, Buddhism, Roman Catholic Christianity, and Sūfīsm (mystic Muhammadanism), and its main features are identical in all. The man who would enter the Path must recognise Unity as his aim, and this is to be reached by profound devotion to God and unwearying service of Man. The first stage is named Purification in the Christian books, the Probationary or Preparatory Path in the others. The Christian name gives the negative side, the getting rid of weaknesses; the non-Christian the positive side, the acquirement of four "Qualifications"; these are: (1) Discrimination between the Real and the Unreal; (2) Dispassion, or Desirelessness as regards the Unreal; (3) the Six Jewels, or Good Conduct, comprising Self-control in Thought, Self-control in Action, Tolerance, Endurance, Confidence in the God within, and Equanimity or Balance; (4) Desire for Union, or Love. The partial but definite acquirement of these by the candidate brings him to the entrance of the Path of Illumination, to use the Christian term, of the Path of Holiness, or "the Path," to use the non-Christian. Theosophy follows the older nomenclature, which divides this Path into four stages, each entered by an "Initiation". Initiation is a definite ceremony, conducted by the Perfected Members of the White Brotherhood, under the sanction of its Head; it gives to the new Initiate an expansion of consciousness, and admits him to a definite rank in the Brotherhood; he is pledged to Service, and is what is technically called "safe for ever"; that is, he cannot drop even temporarily out of evolution during its period of activity.

Each successive Initiation carries with it certain definite obligations, which must be fully discharged before the next step can be taken. The fifth Initiation "perfects" the Man, closing his human evolution. By that He becomes a liberated Spirit; He has "reached the further shore". Some of These remain on our earth, to watch over and forward human evolution; others depart to fill the various offices needed for the helping of our own and other planets, and for the general guidance of the Solar System. Those we call "Masters" are among Those who remain on our earth, and They form the fifth grade of the White Brotherhood; other ranks rise above Them, until the head of the whole Hierarchy is reached.

GOVERNMENT OF OUR WORLD

The world is divided into areas, each of which has a Master at its head, and He guides its activities, selects some men as His instruments, uses them, lays them quietly aside when useless, seeking ever to inspire, to guide, to attract, to check, but never to dominate the human will. The Great Plan must be carried out, but it is carried out by utilising free agents, who pursue certain aims which attract them, power, fame, wealth, and the rest. Where a man's aims, if carried out, will forward the Plan, opportunities to rise are placed in his way, and he obtains what he wants, ignorantly accomplishing a little bit of the Plan. "All the world's a stage, and all the men and women merely players"; but the Drama is written by the divine Playwright; men can only choose their parts, limited in their choice by the Karma they have created in their past, that includes their capacities.

Further, there are great departments in the government of the world, that includes the whole planet. The administrative department, that rules seismic changes, the raising and submerging of continents, the evolution of races, sub-races, and nations, and the like, has among its leading officials the Manus; a Manu is a typical Man, and each root-race has its Manu, embodying its type in its highest perfection.[1] The teaching department is headed by the Bodhisattva, or Christ, the Supreme Teacher of Gods and Men; He founds

[1] See Section VI., "Some Details about Systems and Worlds," pp. 87, 88.

religions directly or through His messengers, and places each under the protection of a Master, He Himself superintending and blessing all. When He becomes a Buddha, He leaves the earth, and is succeeded by another as Bodhisattva.

These Mighty Beings are the vicegerents on our earth of the Supreme Lord, the LOGOS, or manifested God. They are "ministers of His, that do His pleasure". Thus it comes to pass that His world is guided, protected, assisted, as it slowly rolls upwards, by the long road of evolution, to His Feet.

SECTION V

THEOSOPHY APPLIED TO SOCIAL PROBLEMS

IT may help the reader to understand the value of Theosophy in its bearing on Life, if we consider how it may be applied to the resolution of some of the more painful problems which confront us in the present state of Society. Many suggestions may be drawn from civilisations founded and ruled in the past by members of the White Brotherhood, although, under the greatly changed conditions now prevailing, new applications of the fundamental principles must be devised. The foundation of a stable Society must be Brotherhood; the need of every human being is for happiness and for conditions favourable to his evolution, and the duty of Society is to supply an environment which yields these. The birth of a human being into an organised Society gives to him a claim, and to Society a duty—the claim of a child on its parents, the duty of the parents to the child. It is this natural and proper claim of the younger on the elder that has been perverted into the aggressive doctrine of "rights"; animals, children, the sick, the ignorant, the helpless, all these have rights—the right to be kindly used, protected, nursed, taught, shielded; the strong, the grown-up, have only duties.

Organised Society exists for the happiness and the welfare of its members, and where it fails to secure these it stands *ipso facto* condemned. "Government exists only for the good of the governed." So said Pythagoras, preaching on the hill at Tauromenion, and the phrase has echoed down the centuries, and has become the watchword of those who are seeking the betterment of social conditions. Only when the good of the governed is sought and secured does the State deserve the eloquent description with which the great Greek Teacher closed one of his lectures to the Greek colony of Naxos, whose citizens were gathered round him on the hill:

"Listen, my children, to what the State should be to the good citizen. It is more than father or mother, it is more than husband or wife, it is more than child or friend. The State is the father and mother of all, is the wife of the husband, and the husband of the wife. The family is good, and good is the joy of the man in wife and in son. But greater is the State, which is the Protector of all, without which the home would be ravaged and destroyed. Dear to the good man is the honour of the woman who bore him, dear the honour of the wife whose children cling to his knees; but dearer should be the honour of the State that keeps safe the wife and the child. It is the State from which comes all that makes your life prosperous, and gives you beauty and safety. Within the State are built up the Arts, which make the difference between the barbarian and the man. If the brave man dies gladly for the hearthstone, far more gladly should he die for the State."

Pythagoras has become the Master K. H., well known in connection with the Theosophical Society, and he speaks out the Theosophical ideal of the State—the father-mother of its citizens, the Protector of all.

The duty of the State, of organised Society, is to secure to every one of its members at least the minimum of welfare —of food, clothing, shelter, education, leisure—*which will enable each to develop to the full the faculties which he brought with him into the world.* There is no necessity for the existence of starvation and poverty, of overwork and absence of leisure, of lack of comfort and the means of enjoyment. Human brains are quite clever enough to plan out a social system in which every citizen should have enough for happy life; the only obstacles are selfishness and want of will. It was done long ago under the King-Initiates who ruled in the City of the Golden Gate and in Peru. It was done in the time of King Rāmachandra, as may be read in the *Rāmāyana*. It was done when the Manu ruled in the City of the Bridge.[1] But it must be planned out by wisdom, not by ignorance, and brought about by the love and sacrifice of the higher, and not by the uprising of the lower. Mobs can make revolutions; but they cannot build a State.

PRINCIPLES OF THE NEW ORDER

Basing itself on the study of the past, Theosophy can lay down certain principles, to be worked out into details by the highly educated and experienced. The principles are: that Government should be in the hands of the Elders, *i.e.* the wisest, the most experienced, and the morally best; that the possession of ability and of power imposes the duty of service; that freedom brings happiness only to the educated and self-controlled, and that no one, so long as he is ignorant and unself-controlled, should have any share in the governing of others, and should only have such freedom as is consistent with the welfare of the community; that the life of such a one should be rendered as happy and useful as possible, under discipline until he is fit to "run alone," so that his evolution may be quickened; that co-operation, mutual aid, should be substituted for competition, mutual struggle; that the fewer resources a man has within himself, the more means of outer enjoyment should be placed within his reach by Society.

SUGGESTIONS

The suggestions which follow are the results of my own study of what has been done in the past, and of my own thought on present conditions. They are *only*

[1] Much of interest and value may be found on the Manu's policy in Bhagavān Dās' *Science of Social Organisation*.

suggestions, and many Theosophists might disagree with them. My only wish is to indicate a line of change consonant with Theosophical ideas. Brotherhood imperatively demands fundamental social changes, and the rapid growth of unrest, justified by the conditions of the classes that live by manual labour, will force a change ere long. The only question is whether the change shall be brought about by open-eyed wisdom or by blind suffering. At present, Society is engaged in trying the latter plan.

The land of a country should be used to support: (1) the Ruler, his Councillors, Officials of every grade, the administration of Justice, the maintenance of internal Order and of National Defence; (2) Religion, Education, Amusement, Pensions, and the care of the Sick; (3) all who are not included under (1) and (2), and who gain their livelihood by manual labour in production and distribution.

Education, free and universal, should be the only work of the period between seven and twenty-one years of age, so that the youths of both sexes should, on reaching manhood and womanhood, be ready to become dutiful and useful citizens, with their faculties well developed, so that they would be capable of leading an honourable, self-supporting and self-respecting life.

The working life—and all should work in one of the three above-named divisions—should last from twenty-one to fifty years of age, unless a shorter term should be found sufficient for the support of the nation. During the remainder of the life, the citizen should be in receipt of a pension, the result of the accumulated surplus of his working years, and therefore a repayment, not a gift; he should be free to devote himself to any pursuit he pleased.

Production and distribution should be organised by such men as make the huge fortunes now becoming so numerous, and after full provision for all concerned in the producing and distributing, the surplus profits should go to (1) and (2), chiefly to the latter. The organisation of industry should be governed by the idea that labour should be rendered as little burdensome as possible by healthy conditions and by the substitution of machinery for human beings in all unpleasant and dangerous work—mining, drainage, and the like; where unpleasant forms of human labour are necessary for the welfare of the community, the hours of labour should be shortened in proportion to the disagreeableness of the task, without any diminution of pay. If the scavenger, for instance, is to lead a human life, as much of his work as can be done by machinery should be thus performed; for the rest, his hours should be very short, his pay good —since the health of the community depends on him— and recreation, some refining and educative, some purely amusing, should be readily available within his reach. He is an active hand of Nature, helping her in her constant task of transforming the foul and the dangerous into the nourishment of new life and new beauty. He should be regarded, as said on p. 34. not as a drudge but as a co-worker with God. Is it said that he is coarse, repellent? So much the more shame for us, the refined and attractive, who profit by his work, and have made him what he is by our selfishness, our indifference, and our neglect.

The doctrine of Reincarnation, applied to education, leads us to see in the child an ego who has come into our care during the time of the growth of his body, to be helped in training it for the purpose for which he has returned to the earth. Recognising that in the ego himself are enshrined all the powers accumulated in past lives, and that the germs of these are planted in the new mental body, we feel the full force of Plato's famous phrase, that "All knowledge is reminiscence," and seek to draw out of the ego that which he knows, that he may stimulate the germinal mental faculties, and so impress the plastic brain. We do not regard the child-body as belonging to us, parents or teachers, but as belonging to the ego, and we see it to be our duty to help him in gaining full possession of it, to work from outside while he works from within, and to follow out any indication given by him as to the best line of study, the easiest road of progress. We give to the child the greatest liberty compatible with his physical, moral, and mental safety, and in everything try to understand and to help, not to coerce. The detailed application of these principles may be read in an admirable little book on *Education and Service*, by Alcyone.

Reincarnation, applied to the treatment of criminals and of the undeveloped class which is ever on the verge of crime, suggests a policy wholly different from that of our present Society, which gives them complete liberty to do as they like, punishes them when they commit a legal offence, restores them to liberty after a varying term of gaol, and so gives them a life of alternating freedom and imprisonment, transforming them into habitual criminals, and handing them over finally to "the divine mercy," man having failed to do any good with them.[1] In the light of Reincarnation I suggest that the congenital criminal is a savage, come to us as to a school, and that it is our business to treat him as the intellectual and moral baby which he is, and to restrain the wild beast in him from doing harm. These people, and the almost criminal class above them, are recognisable from birth, and they should be segregated in small special schools, given such elementary education as they can assimilate, be treated kindly and firmly, have many games, and be taught a rough form of manual labour. The teachers in these schools should be volunteers from the higher social classes, willing to teach and play with the boys, and capable of arousing in them a feeling of admiration, attachment, and loyalty, which would evoke obedience. They must be with those who are obviously their superiors if this is to be done. From these schools they should be drafted into small colonies, bright, pleasant villages, with shops, playground, music-hall, and restaurant, ruled by men of the same type as

[1] That which follows is the immediate treatment of the criminal as he is. We hope, later, to eliminate the type.

before; they should have everything to make life pleasant, except freedom to make it mischievous and miserable; these colonies would supply gangs of labourers for all the rougher kinds of work, mining, road-making, porterage, scavengering, etc., leaving the decent people now employed in these free for higher tasks. Some, the true congenital criminal, the raw savage, would remain under this kindly restraint for life, but they would go out of life far less of savages than they were when they came into it. Some would respond to the treatment, and would acquire sufficient industry and self-control to be ultimately set free. The chief difficulties would be innate rowdyism and idleness, for the criminal is a loafer, incapable of steady industry. The school would do something to improve him, and to do right would be made pleasant, while to be rowdy and idle would be made unpleasant; "he that will not work neither shall he eat" is a sound maxim, for food is made by work, and he who, being able, refuses to make it has no claim to it. Checks might be given for each hour's work, exchangeable at the shops and restaurant for the necessaries of life, and the man could do as much or as little as he liked; the equivalent in necessaries and luxuries would be at his own choice. It is only possible here to indicate the broad lines of the solution of this problem, and similar methods would be employed, *mutatis mutandis*, with girls and women of the corresponding type.

Karma, applied to the slums, would see in them magnets for the lowest types of incarnating Spirits; it would be our wisdom, as it is our duty, to get rid of these foul spots, attractive only to the most undesirable of the incoming crowd. In the light of Theosophy, it is the duty of the elders to plan out, and gradually to construct, towns of decent dwellings with sufficient interspaces, to which should be transplanted the dwellers in the slums; these poison-spots must be pulled down, and the soil, sodden with the filth of generations, should be turned into gardens; the filth will then be changed into trees and flowers, whereas to build new houses on such soil is to invite disease. Moreover, Beauty must be sought, for, as said in Section II., it is a necessity of life for all, not a luxury for the few. Beauty refines and cultivates, and reproduces itself in the forms and manners of those who live under its influences. Beauty in dress, in the home, in the town, is a crying need as an evolutionary force. It is not without significance that before the present age of machinery, when people were more surrounded by natural beauty than they are now, the clothes of the people of every class were beautiful, as they still are in the East; it is natural to man to seek to express himself in Beauty; it is only as he becomes far removed from Nature, that he accepts with indifference ugliness in clothes and surroundings. Contrast the clothes seen in our slums with those seen in an Indian village.

Volumes might be written on this theme of the application of Theosophy to life, but within our present limits the above must suffice.

SECTION VI

A Few Details about Systems and Worlds

In Section III. the basic principle of the relation between Spirit and Matter was given. It may be interesting to consider some of its details.

It is possible to see that the universal Æther within our Solar System—and presumably elsewhere, since there are many such Systems—contains innumerable bubbles, exactly similar in appearance to bubbles arising *within* water, empty spaces, walled in only by the surrounding water. A soap-bubble floating in the air is a tiny portion of air within a surrounding film of soapy water; but the bubbles in water are tiny portions of air within a mass of water, and have no limiting film; they are kept as bubbles by the pressure of the water containing them. So these bubbles are kept as bubbles by the pressure of the surrounding Æther, and as they cannot escape from this, they can only remain bubbles. They are "holes in Æther," or, as H. P. Blavatsky called them long ago, "holes in Space," and she said that they were made by "Fohat," the power of the Supreme Logos. Ancient books similarly speak of "the great Breath" as their cause; the analogy is obvious, since bubbles may be produced by breathing into water. A French scientist, quoted by Mr. Leadbeater,[1] says: "There is no matter; there are nothing but holes in the ether." But out of the aggregations of these holes, all that we call matter is built up.

[1] *A Text-Book of Theosophy*, p. 27

THE BUILDING OF ATOMS BY THE FIRST LIFE-WAVE

The LOGOS of a Solar System encloses a huge fragment of the universal Æther, thus bubble-filled, within His before-mentioned Ring-Pass-Not. The bubbles are visible to the sight of the third or spiritual sphere, and one can see that He sets up a great whirl of force, which sweeps the bubbles together into a huge mass; the Third Aspect of the LOGOS is the Creative, and through this He sends forth the first Life-Wave, as it is called, which builds the bubbles into atoms, later aggregates atoms into molecules, and finally builds these into the six familiar sets of combinations, which in the physical world are called sub-atomic, super-etheric, etheric, gaseous, liquid, and solid.

These original separate bubbles form the matter of the divine sphere, while that of the monadic sphere is made of groupings of the bubbles into atoms, these being formed by an impulse of the Life-Wave of Creative Thought, causing minute vortices, each of which draws in 49 bubbles; thus two interpenetrating worlds are formed, the divine and the monadic, the first of free bubbles, the second of some of these combined into atoms, each atom consisting of 49 bubbles. The second impulse from the Life-Wave separates out a quantity of these 49-atom-bubbles, dissociates them, and recombines them in vortices, each of which contains 49^2 bubbles, the atoms of the spiritual world. A third impulse separates a mass of these from the remainder, dissociates them, and recombines them in vortices, each of which contains 49^3 bubbles, the atoms of the intuitional world. A fourth impulse in similar fashion yields atoms of the mental world, containing 49^4 bubbles. A fifth yields atoms of the astral world, containing 49^5 bubbles, and a sixth builds the atoms of the physical world, each composed of 49^6 bubbles. Thus are formed the interpenetrating spheres of seven types of matter, each type being the atomic basis of a world composed entirely of combinations of its own particular atom. When this series of atoms was complete, the seventh impulse was sent forth, and this built aggregations of atoms, a vast number of different combinations; these again entered into further combinations with each other, in the process of many ages, a period of inconceivable length; during this time the glowing nebula gradually cooled, ultimately being broken up into a central Sun, with various planets revolving round him as centre. This is the vast work of the Creative Aspect of the Solar LOGOS, the "Spirit of God" who "moved upon the face of the waters" of Æther, the axis of the whirling mountain which churned up the ocean, so that out of it living things might arise.

THE RELATION BETWEEN ATOMS AND CONSCIOUSNESS

There is one point of great interest in the formation of atoms that ought not to be omitted. The Life of the LOGOS is the whirling force within the atom, that holds its component parts together. This Life gives to the atom its distinctive quality, its essential nature, which is a particular mode of the divine Consciousness; the Hindū calls this the "tattva," literally the "Thatness"; "Tat," "That," is a reverent expression for the Divine Being, and Thatness indicates "Godness," or "God-nature". Each atom has thus its "Godness". The measure of the vibration of the atom, imposed upon it by the Will of the LOGOS, is the "tanmātra," the "measure of That"; this is the axes of the atom,[1] lines of the thought-force of the LOGOS, the angular divergence of which, within the fixed limits of vibration, determines its surface form. Each type of atom has its own peculiar work, for the states of consciousness manifested by the LOGOS within His universe—what He is outside it none, save His peers, can tell—are

[1] Like the axes of crystals. They are "imaginary" lines; but imagination is the creative power, and these lines govern the form of the crystal, though they are "non-existent".

identical in quality, though not in quantity, with the states of consciousness in Man, the faint image of His glory. It is thus His consciousness within the atom which answers to our consciousness, stage by stage, the material of the atom faithfully reflecting each stage in the wave-lengths of its vibrations. Thus the atom of the spiritual world vibrates in answer to the modes of Spirit—Spirit being its life; that of the intuitional world to the modes of Intuition—for a like reason; that of the mental world to the modes of Intellect; that of the emotional world to the modes of Emotion and Passion; that of the physical world to the modes of Vitality—all for like reasons. Each change in consciousness in any of these states is at once answered by a change of vibration in the corresponding matter; any vibration set up in matter is at once answered by a change in the corresponding state of consciousness. For instance, all the matter of the emotional, or astral, sphere is composed of atoms, the Life in which is Emotion, and the measure of vibration of which is correlated to emotion, to express and respond to it. The whole huge gamut of emotions, passions, desires, is played by consciousness on this matter, and pure passion and desire on this matter only; as emotion is a mingling of passion and thought, some mingling of thought-matter enters into the expression of emotion. The matter of the mental sphere is made of atoms similarly connected with thought; the Life is Mentality, the measure of vibration is correlated to thought, to express and respond to it. As definitely as in the physical world the range of sounds lies within certain vibration-numbers, and the range of colours within others, so can thoughts and passions only be expressed by matter which vibrates within certain limits.

Chains

When this part of the work has proceeded sufficiently far for planets to be possible within the Solar System, a series of six globes composed of the matter of the spheres of varying densities is formed in connection with each planet—seven globes, including the planet. Such a series is called a Chain, and during its period of evolution it passes through seven stages, or lives; there is thus a succession of seven Chains, and this complete series is termed a Scheme of Evolution, and is under the charge of a mighty spiritual Intelligence, called by Theosophists a "Ruler of seven Chains".[1] There are ten of these in our Solar System, but only seven are in manifestation, ruled by the "seven Spirits before the throne of God," mentioned in the "Revelation of S. John". They are at different stages of evolution, marked by the sphere of matter in which their lowest globes exist. Thus the Neptunian and the Terrene Chains have each three globes in the physical sphere, for these are both at their deepest point of descent into matter, in their middle, or fourth, life. The seven globes of the Earth Chain include Mars, the Earth, and Mercury; those of the Neptunian, Neptune and his two satellites.

Those who are interested in this part of Theosophical study must pursue it in larger books, for it is naturally very complicated.

THE BUILDING OF FORMS BY THE SECOND LIFE-WAVE

Let us consider our own Chain. Evolution circles round a Chain seven times, and each of these cycles is appropriately called a Round. The evolutionary force is called the Second Life-Wave, and it is the Life which is sent out by the Logos through His second Aspect of Wisdom, the dual Aspect, Knowledge-Love. Speaking generally, this Life-Wave descends through the spheres of matter, causing ever-increasing differentiation, and then returns, causing reintegration into unity. Its first work is to give to matter certain qualities, fitting it to be materials for bodies; it pours itself into the three

[1] Called also a Planetary Logos, but the name causes confusion.

finer kinds of matter which form the higher mental sphere; matter thus infused with the second Life-Wave is called, when atomic, "Monadic Essence," because it has become fit to be used to supply permanent atoms to Monads;[1] when non-atomic, *i.e.* molecular, matter is used, it is called "Elemental Essence"—a name borrowed from the writings of mediæval Occultists; it was bestowed by them on the matter of which the bodies of nature-spirits were composed, for they spoke of these as "Elementals," dividing them into classes belonging to the "Elements" of Air, Fire, Water, and Earth. The three higher levels of the mental sphere are, regarded as mental Elemental Essence, the "first Elemental Kingdom". All abstract "thought-forms" made of this, and a large and splendid host of Angels—Bodiless Devas—have bodies composed of this matter. The four lower levels of the mental sphere, suffused by the second Life-Wave, form the "second Elemental Kingdom"; of this are made the bodies of the lower Angels—Form Devas. When the Life-Wave enters the astral world, the atomic matter becomes astral Monadic Essence, and the molecular matter astral Elemental Essence, the "third Elemental Kingdom"; the bodies of the lowest Angels—Passion Devas—and of very many nature-spirits are composed of this. The Life-Wave passes on into the physical world, and performs its accustomed task; the bodies of the lower nature-spirits, fairies, gnomes, and the like, are made of the etheric matter thus suffused. The Mineral Kingdom is the turning-point of density; there the second half of the work of the Life-Wave proceeds, the building up of the bodies, plants, animals, and men, now on the ascending arc; the astral and mental bodies are also built of the Elemental Essence on this ascending arc. Hence the conflict that often arises between the life of the man and the life in the matter of his bodies. The latter is pressing downwards, seeking grosser and grosser embodiment and sharper differentiation; the former is

[1] See Section I., p. 24.

aspiring upwards, and is seeking unity. S. Paul naturally exclaims as to this conflict: "I find another law in my members, warring against the law of my mind, and bringing me into captivity to the law of sin which is in my members." The Man must bring "the flesh" into subjection, for its life is evolutionarily downwards, on the descending arc, and his is evolutionarily upwards, on the ascending arc, taking its way to the realisation of Spirit.

THE COMING OF THE MONAD BY THE THIRD LIFE-WAVE

The point at which Man definitely "individualises," is when the Monad and his Ray—Spirit, Intuition, and Intellect—who had been brooding over the evolving forms carried in the bosom of the second Life-Wave, flashes downwards to meet the evolving embodied life, and the causal body is formed of the matter of the first Elemental Kingdom, on the higher levels of the mental sphere. The human Monads are also borne on a divine current, the "third Life-Wave," coming forth from the LOGOS through His first Aspect. We see, then, that the LOGOS sends forth three mighty waves of His Life, through His three Aspects in succession: the first shapes and ensouls matter; the second imparts qualities and builds forms; the third carries down the human Monad to unite with the forms prepared by the second.

ROOT-RACES AND SUB-RACES

We must now narrow our attention to our own world. Three times has evolution swept round the series of globes of which our earth is the densest—three Rounds lie behind us. The fourth sweep has come as far as our earth, which is now evolving under its influence. Minerals, plants, animals, men, all evolve together, but we may confine ourselves to men. Seven root-types of men evolve on our earth during this stage of its life. Theosophists call these types Root-Races, and each has its own special "continent," or configuration of land. The first two Root-Races have disappeared. Of the third, the Lemurian, which flourished on the continent of Lemuria, now beneath the Pacific Ocean for the most part, scarcely a pure specimen remains; the negroes are its descendants from mixed marriages. The fourth, the Atlantean, spread over the earth from the continent of Atlantis, which united western Europe and Africa with eastern America; it built some of the mightiest civilisations the world has known, and the greater part of the world's inhabitants still belong to it. The fifth, the Āryan, leads humanity to-day. The sixth is in the womb of the future, but its continent is beginning its formation, and will occupy, roughly, the Lemurian site; the islands now being thrown up in the northern Pacific are the indications of the commencement of a work which will demand hundreds of thousands of years for its accomplishment. The seventh lies far, far ahead.

Each Root-Race divides into seven sub-races; we have the fourth Root-Race divided into the Rmoahal, Tlavatli, Toltec, Turanian, Semitic, Akkadian, and Mongolian sub-races. The fifth Root-Race has, so far, produced five sub-races: the Hindū, Arabian, Iranian, Keltic, and Teutonic; the sixth sub-race is beginning to show itself in the United States.

Each Root-Race has, as the shaper of its type and the guardian of its evolution, a Great Being called a "Manu"; the name is derived from *man*, to think, the root of "man," "homme," "mann," etc. The Manu is *The* Man, the type-Man of a Root-Race. The great racial types may be realised by putting side by side a Negro, a Mongol, an Āryan. The sub-race differences are shown by a German and an Italian.

It will be seen that immense subjects of study are here opened up, profoundly interesting, though not bearing immediately on human happiness and human conduct.

SECTION VII

The Theosophical Society

The Theosophical Society was founded in 1875 by a Russian, Helena Petrovna Blavatsky, and an American, Henry Steele Olcott. The first brought to it her vast occult knowledge and entire self-sacrifice—she belonged to a wealthy family of the Russian nobility; the second brought extraordinary organising ability, already proved in his service to his country in the purification of its military department during the Civil War. At first, on their reassertion of the Ancient Wisdom in the modern world, they met a whirlwind of ridicule and contempt. Now the ideas have spread into every civilised country, and it may be said, without fear of contradiction, that it is to-day influencing the whole world of thought.

The basis of the Society is a little peculiar; only one thing is binding on every member—the acceptance of Universal Brotherhood.

Its objects are:

First.—To form a nucleus of the Universal Brotherhood of Humanity, without distinction of race, creed, sex, caste, or colour.

Second.—To encourage the study of comparative religion, philosophy, and science.

Third.—To investigate the unexplained laws of Nature and the powers latent in man.

It will be seen that no member is asked either to believe or to spread Theosophical teachings. Every member is left absolutely free to study exactly as he chooses; he may accept or reject any Theosophical teaching; he remains in his own religion, Hindū, Parsī, Buddhist, Hebrew, Christian, Muhammadan, and his religion, if he holds to it strongly, will colour all his ideas. If he accepts Theosophical teachings, a strong believer in any special form of religion will present them in his own form, and is absolutely free to do so. But he must not insist on his own form of them being accepted by others.

The experiment of forming a profoundly religious body open to members of all religions equally is a unique one, but it is gradually succeeding, with many difficulties, occasional friction between members holding strongly to opposing views, and plenty of discussion as to details. The main policy of perfect tolerance, and the reason for the policy, have been formulated as follows by myself, and have been objected to by no member. It may, therefore, be presented as stating the general view.

No person's religious opinions are asked upon his joining, nor is interference with them permitted, but everyone is required to show to the religion of his fellow-members the same respect as he claims for his own.

The Society has no dogmas, and therefore no heretics. It does not shut any man out because he does not believe the Theosophical teachings. A man may deny every one of them, save that of human Brotherhood, and claim his place and his right within its ranks.

Theosophists realise that just because the intellect can only do its best work in its own atmosphere of freedom, truth can best be seen when no conditions are laid down as to the right of investigation, as to the methods of research. To them Truth is so supreme a thing, that they do not desire to bind any man with conditions as to how, or where, or why he shall seek it.

The future of the Society depends on the fact that it should include a vast variety of opinions on all questions on which differences of opinion exist; it is not desirable that there should be within it only one school of thought, and it is the duty of every member to guard this liberty for himself and for others. The Theosophical Society is the servant of the Divine Wisdom, and its motto is: "There is no Religion higher than Truth". It seeks in every error for the heart of truth whereby it lives, and whereby it attaches to itself human minds.

Every religion, every philosophy, every science, every activity, draws what it has of truth and beauty from the Divine Wisdom, but cannot claim it as exclusively its own, or as against others. Theosophy does not belong to the Theosophical Society; the Theosophical Society belongs to Theosophy.

The Theosophical Society is composed of students, belonging to any religion in the world or to none, who are united by their approval of the above objects, by their wish to remove religious antagonisms and to draw together men of goodwill, whatsoever their religious opinions, and by their desire to study religious truths and to share the results of their studies with others. Their bond of union is not the profession of a common belief, but a common search and aspiration for Truth. They hold that Truth should be sought by study, by reflection, by purity of life, by devotion to high ideals, and they regard Truth as a prize to be striven for, not as a dogma to be imposed by authority. They consider that belief should be the result of individual study or intuition, and not its antecedent, and should rest on knowledge, not on assertion. They extend tolerance to all, even to the intolerant, not as a privilege they bestow but as a duty they perform, and they seek to remove ignorance, not to punish it. They see every religion as a partial expression of the Divine Wisdom, and prefer its study to its condemnation, and its practice to proselytism. Peace is their watchword, as Truth is their aim.

Theosophy is the body of truths which forms the basis of all religions, and which cannot be claimed as the exclusive possession of any. Members of the Theosophical Society study these truths, and Theosophists endeavour to live them. Everyone willing to study, to be tolerant, to aim high, and to work perseveringly, is welcomed as a member, and it rests with the member to become a true Theosophist.

I may add that most of us regard the Theosophical Society as the result of a spiritual impulse, sent out by the White Brotherhood, in order to save the world from sinking into Materialism, and to prepare the minds of men for the restoration of the esoteric teachings of religion. It is to us the latest of many such impulses, the earlier ones being embodied in separate religions, while this seeks to draw the existing religions into united friendly co-operation. We regard H. P. Blavatsky as a Messenger of the White Brotherhood, and many of us, I myself among the number, feel to her the deepest gratitude, because she opened to us, in this life, the gateway through which we have passed into the presence of Those who sent her.

BIBLIOGRAPHY

H. P. Blavatsky, *The Secret Doctrine.*
— *The Key to Theosophy.*
— *The Voice of the Silence.*
A. P. Sinnett, *Esoteric Buddhism.*
— *The Occult World.*
— *The Growth of the Soul.*
Annie Besant, *The Ancient Wisdom.*
— *A Study in Consciousness.*
— *Thought-Power.*
— *An Introduction to Yoga.*
— *Esoteric Christianity.*
— *The Laws of the Higher Life.*
— *In the Outer Court.*
— *The Path of Discipleship.*
— *Initiation, the Perfecting of Man.*
— *The Three Paths and Dharma.*
— *Universal Text-Book of Religion and Morals.*
Annie Besant and C. W. Leadbeater, *Thought-Forms.*
— *Occult Chemistry.*
— *Man: Whence, How, Whither.*
C. W. Leadbeater, *Man Visible and Invisible.*
— *The Other Side of Death.*
— *Some Glimpses of Occultism.*
— *The Inner Life*, 2 vols.
— *Invisible Helpers.*
— *Clairvoyance.*
— *A Text-Book of Theosophy.*
J. Krishnamurti, *At the Feet of the Master.*
— *Education as Service.*
Bhagavān Dās, *The Science of the Emotions.*
— *The Science of Peace.*
— *The Science of Social Organisation.*
Mabel Collins, *Light on the Path.*
H. S. Olcott, *Old Diary Leaves, a History of the Theosophical Society.*

INDEX

PRINTED IN GREAT BRITAIN.